DISCARDED

Your One-Stop
Guide to
How Saints Are Made

Your One-Stop Guide to How Saints Are Made

BILL DODDS

CHARIS

SERVANT PUBLICATIONS
ANN ARBOR, MICHIGAN

Charis Books is an imprint of Servant Publications especially designed to serve
Roman Catholics.

Excerpts from the English translation of the *Catechism of the Catholic Church* for
the United States of America. Copyright © 1994, United States Catholic
Conference, Inc.-Libreria Editrice Vaticana. Used with permission.

Servant Publications
P.O. Box 8617
Ann Arbor, MI 48107

Cover design: Hile Illustration and Design, Ann Arbor, Michigan

00 01 02 03 10 9 8 7 6 5 4 3 2 1

Printed in the United States of America
ISBN 1-56955-198-7

LIBRARY OF CONGRESS CATALOGING-IN-PUBLICATION DATA

Dodds, Bill.
    Your one-stop guide to how saints are made / Bill Dodds.
        p.   cm.
    Includes bibliographical references and index.
    ISBN 1-56955-198-7 (alk. paper)
    1. Christian saints.   2. Canonization.   3. Catholic Church—Doctrines.
    I. Title.

    BX2325.D58   2000
    235'.24—dc21   00-031437

Dedication

For Monica

Contents

A Few Warnings

In many ways an introduction is just a series of disclaimers and warnings. These are mine:

—While some saints were somber, others enjoyed a laugh as much as anyone else. *Your One-Stop Guide to How Saints Are Made* uses a light touch but, I hope, never a disrespectful one. It's an attitude I inherited, adopted or received genetically from my dad, John J. Dodds (who, I believe, is having a fun time in heaven even as you read these words).

—You may already know some of the material presented here so I've broken chapters into sections that can easily be read or ignored. Each chapter has a main "article" and then a number of "sidebars" or related articles. These "links" are marked with "Go to" in the main article or in sidebars.

—The years listed after a pope are his time in office (his "reign"), not his life span. "Pope Gregory (590–604)" didn't die at fourteen.

—Don't be intimidated if you never cared for history (and, in school, it never seemed to care for you). I'm sure historians would be the first to tell you, "Well, this certainly isn't a *history* book. At least, not like one I've ever ..."

—Don't worry about being disappointed if you've always loved history (and, in school, it loved you right back). I'm sure non-history buffs would be the first to tell you, "Well, this certainly has names of dead people and a bunch about other old stuff."

—I've asked the saints for their help as I wrote this book and I think they provided some. Even so, any mistakes are entirely my own.

—I've asked them to help you, too, as you read it. I believe they will.

—You—singular; yes, you—have the potential to become a saint.

CHAPTER ONE

What Is a Saint and Why Should I Care If the Church Makes Them?

"St. Mary Mag Demolishes St. Pete"

Years ago I was interviewing a group of folks for a newspaper article. Some of them were Catholic, some not. When I asked one where he lived in Seattle, he replied, "Capitol Hill."

"Oh," I said, "St. Joe's," and he nodded.

"'St. Joe's'?" another person—a non-Catholic—interrupted. "Isn't that a little ... informal."

The two of us looked startled. I hadn't meant to be disrespectful. It was just a form of Catholic shorthand. Double shorthand, really.

First, Catholics have divided the entire world into parishes and so sometimes streets or sections of town don't matter. It's easier to say, "We used to live in Omaha. The cathedral." Or, "I didn't know you were from Jersey City. My mother-in-law's family was from St. Paul's."

And second, being associated with a particular saint at a parish, school or institution tends to breed a certain level of comfort. If a nickname is possible, eventually it gets used. Little kids shout, "Go, St. Pat's," at Catholic Youth Organization games. (And the local Catholic weekly duly reports, "St. Pat Crushes Lady of the Lake.") Their older brothers and sisters attend a high school commonly referred to as "St. Bart's." Their mother or father is on the staff at a hospital known as "St. Al's."

By the time a person reaches adulthood, both the habit and the geographical designations can be ingrained.

Saints as Weirdos

But who said Pat was a saint? Who decided Bart or Al deserved a halo? And what about Our Lady of the Lake? If the Blessed Mother is a saint, why isn't she referred to as St. Mary instead of just plain Mary? (In fact, there are some places where she is, but it's not too common. The Church says she is worthy of a particular form of veneration. We'll talk about that in chapter two.)

Cradle Catholics—those baptized as infants—can grow up thinking "that's just the way things are." And incorrectly assume that's just the way things have always been. Converts—who join the Church when they're older—have a tendency to put sainthood into the "It's One of Those Catholic Things" file.

An even more basic question is, what *is* a saint? Sometimes our images and our own definitions can be rather skewed. (Now, there's a polite word. Our images or definitions can be downright cockamamie.) We accumulate them from a variety of sources, some reliable, some off-the-wall. It's not that a well-meaning relative, teacher or pastor wanted to spread legendary misinformation. It's more that their explanation of sainthood wasn't accurate. Or how we interpreted their explanation was fuzzy. (Like a photocopy of a photocopy of a photocopy.)

We might think saints are:

1. Really angels in human bodies. Or humans who become angels after they die.
2. Holy Joes and Janes who never sinned.

3. So far beyond us there's no hope of our ever reaching their level.

4. Folks who would have behaved differently if they had had much-needed professional psychiatric help.

5. Just plain weird.

But ...

— Angels are angels and humans are humans. After a person dies, he or she doesn't become an angel.

— Every saint sinned. Every single one. And some were big-time sinners before they changed their ways. (And even after they changed their ways, none were perfect. Folks who lived with saints have reported that it wasn't always a picnic being part of their inner circle.) In all history, there have been only two people who didn't sin. Jesus, God made man. And his mother, Mary.

— Every person has the God-given potential to become a saint. Every single one of us. Including you. And me.

— Some saints did suffer tremendous psychological and emotional problems. Some suffered physical ailments. All used whatever suffering came their way to make them better and more loving people. None endured any kind of pain—either psychological, emotional or physical—because they were masochists. Masochism is not a virtue.

— It could be said that saints are just plain weird and have always been considered just plain weird when compared with what the world considers normal. If the goals and successes of the world are used as the "square," then saints are way off-kilter. And Jesus was pretty much sideways.

So What Is a Saint?

The Church has recognized holy men and women as saints since apostolic times *and* has continued to develop its teaching about them even up to our own time. Not too long ago Pope John Paul II made some big changes in how saints are "made." (We'll talk about that in chapter four.)

He was also the one who saw to it that the Church produced a catechism in the early 1990s. He knew many Catholics had a spotty education when it comes to what the Church teaches. And he knew many of them wanted to know what's what.

Many if not most older Catholics—those who began their schooling before the Second Vatican Council—cut their teeth on the Baltimore Catechism. ("Catechism" means a summary, usually in the form of questions and answers.) It had been around, in the United States, since the end of the nineteenth century.

While the Baltimore Catechism was written for children, the new *Catechism of the Catholic Church* is designed for adults. So now we have a definitive resource to help us learn what the Church teaches and to dispel misinformation.

A saint, it tells us, is a "disciple who has lived a life of exemplary fidelity to the Lord" [2156]. That could be someone who was world famous or extremely obscure. Someone who lived in poverty or riches. Someone who was never sick a day in his life or never healthy. Male or female. Adult or child. Of any race. From any land. Married, single, professed or ordained. Brilliant or simple. The variations go on and on because the list of saints goes on and on.

At its root, that's what being "canonized" means. Here

"canon" refers to a list (or roll or register). In this case it's a list or calendar of holy people who the Church declares have made it to heaven. "By *canonizing* some of the faithful, i.e., by solemnly proclaiming that they practiced heroic virtue and lived in fidelity to God's grace ..." the *Catechism* says, "... the Church recognizes the power of the Spirit of holiness within her and sustains the hope of believers by proposing the saints to them as models and intercessors" [828].[1]

In other words, a saint isn't someone who was just a good person. Or even a really good person. It is a person who was heroically good. Someone who was outstanding.

But human. Always human. And what these people did, the Church teaches, we also have the potential to accomplish.

So, in one sense, the Church "makes" saints by the canonization process. Or in the case of those who died before the current process was in place, it approved a devotion that was already going strong. But that process is nothing more, and nothing less, than simply recognizing the grace-filled, holy lives these people lived.

OK, but What's in It for Me?

Why should you care if the Church makes saints? Why should you care that there even *are* saints? What's in it for you?

There are a couple of ways to look at that. The first is very practical. It never hurts to have friends in high places. That's true in any situation.

And the second is spiritual. Because of the "communion of saints" (*Go to: "You Are Part of the Communion of Saints"*), these Christian all-stars can help you. Here is a treasure, a powerhouse, just waiting to be tapped by anyone who wants to tap it. Anywhere, anytime. All you have to do is ask.

You Are Part of the Communion of Saints

It's a phrase in a prayer called the Apostles' Creed. Near the end. "I believe in the Communion of Saints, the forgiveness of sins, the resurrection of the body and life everlasting. Amen."

Forgiveness of sins is easy to define. Resurrection of the body means that, at the end of time, our souls will be reunited with our bodies. "Life everlasting"? No problem. But what is the "Communion of Saints"?

Maybe we should start with what it *isn't*. It isn't the saints receiving Holy Communion in heaven. No, here *communion* means a sharing. And it means us. All of us. The saints in heaven, the faithful on earth and the souls in purgatory. (*Go to: "Heaven, Hell and Purgatory: What They Are ... and Aren't."*) In old-time lingo this trio was known as the Church triumphant, the Church militant and the Church suffering.

In *Lumen Gentium* (The Dogmatic Constitution on the Church), the bishops at the Second Vatican Council described the Communion of Saints as "the living communion that exists between us and our brothers who are in the glory of heaven and who are yet to be purified after their death." And, of course, by "brothers" they mean brothers and sisters.

The Church teaches that we can pray *to* and *for* the dead. And they can pray for us. But is praying to them a form of idolatry? No. It's simply asking for their help—for their prayers, for their "intercession"—the same way that we might ask a relative or friend to do that for us here and now. ("I've got a killer test tomorrow. Say a prayer for me.")

The *Catechism of the Catholic Church* talks about the Apostles' Creed specifically and it asks, "What is the Church if not the assembly of all the saints?"[2] And "The communion of saints is the Church" [946].

It goes on to say, "Since all the faithful form one body, the good of each is communicated to the others.... We must therefore believe there exists a communion of goods in the Church. But the most important member is Christ, since he is the head.... Therefore, the riches of Christ are communicated to all the members, through the sacraments" [947].[3] This means that the saints in heaven are a source for leading us to Christ, *the* source.

There are a couple of things here to pay particular attention to.

First, anyone who has died, not just a person canonized by the Church, can intercede for us. Just as we can ask the canonized saints to help us, we can ask the same of our departed loved ones. They, too, are members of the Communion of Saints.

And second, this means we can continue to love family and friends who have died and *they can continue to love us.* Death cannot stop or conquer love.

In the Communion of Saints, the *Catechism* says, "a perennial link of charity exists between the faithful who have already reached their heavenly home, those who are expiating their sins in purgatory and those who are still pilgrims on earth" [1475].[4]

Between these, "there is ... an abundant exchange of all good things."[5] The "holiness of one profits others, well beyond the harm that the sin of one could cause others" [1475].

The good outweighs the bad.

Heaven, Hell and Purgatory: What They Are ... and Aren't

In 1999 Pope John Paul II gave a series of talks on heaven, hell and purgatory. He explained:

Heaven "is not an abstraction, not a physical place amid the clouds, but a living and personal relationship with the Holy Trinity."

Hell, "more than a place, ... is the situation in which one finds himself after freely and definitively withdrawing from God, the source of life and joy."

And "before we enter into God's kingdom, every trace of sin within us must be eliminated, every imperfection in our soul must be corrected.... This is exactly what takes place in purgatory."

Heaven is being with God, "face-to-face."

Hell is saying "no" to God and choosing to not be with him.

Purgatory is where a person learns to become better at loving.

A few more points on that last spot, since it's the one with which you might be least familiar:

The Church says if you "die in God's grace and friend-ship"—you've been a good person but had some nasty moments, too—then you're imperfectly purified. You haven't developed your ability to love. You haven't demonstrated that love to the degree that you really should have.

If that's the case, then you still need to undergo purifi-cation "to achieve the holiness necessary to enter the joy of heaven."

The Church formulated this doctrine or teaching at the Councils of Florence (1431–1445) and Trent (1545–1563). It's also based on the practice of praying for the dead, a traditional Christian custom that was mentioned in the Old Testament. Praying for the dead is based on Scripture: "Therefore [Judas Maccabeus] made atonement for the dead, that they might be delivered from their sin." That comes from 2 Maccabees 12:46.

So why don't Protestants accept it? Because that book, along with several others, isn't part of the "canon" or list of books in the Protestant Bible. In the sixteenth century Martin Luther decided some books didn't belong on the reformed list and 2 Maccabees was one of them.

But then, too, in Luther's day the linking of purgatory with indulgences was way out of line. This isn't to say there are no such things as indulgences. (*Go to: "Indulgences Are Still Around."*) The Church still recommends "almsgiving, indulgences, and works of penance undertaken on behalf of the dead."

At the time of the Reformation, the problem was that indulgences were being marketed as get-out-of-purgatory passes. Come up with enough coin, and your departed loved one passes right through the Pearly Gates.

Clearly, that wasn't right.

Worse still, some people were pushing indulgences as get-into-heaven-free cards. Buy one now, be as rotten as you want for the rest of your life and your salvation is assured.

Clearly, that was wrong. But, understandably, very popular in some circles.

Indulgences Are Still Around

It's easy to misunderstand what indulgences are all about. And it's easy to dismiss them as some quaint, outdated custom. (Like writing with a quill pen.)

So hang in there for this section because indulgences are:

a) Still around.

b) Still valuable.

Here are six things to keep in mind:

1. An indulgence is a remission before God of the temporal punishment due to sins whose guilt has already been forgiven. This means sins that have already been confessed and absolved. We'll look more closely at the first part of this in just a moment.

2. They can be partial or "plenary"—complete.

3. They can be gained only for oneself or for the souls in purgatory, but not for another living person.

4. Indulgences are "derived." They come from what is called "the treasury of merits" of the saints, from Jesus and from Mary. Crudely put, we all belong to the same spiritual co-op, and what they have put into it is available to us under particular conditions.

5. You may have seen "100 days indulgence" or "300 days indulgence" written in small type after a prayer. That means saying that prayer, or performing some act, is the equivalent to that amount of time performing penance in the ancient Church. (In the old days, penances given during confession could be more than a few Our Fathers or Hail Marys.) As recently as 1999 a revised

"Enchiridion Indulgentiarum," or manual of indulgences, was released by the Vatican.

6. If you die immediately after receiving a plenary indulgence, you skip purgatory.

OK, let's take a closer look at the first part of number one.

"A remission before God": A pardon, a forgiveness, in God's eyes.

"Of the temporal punishment due to sin": We need to explain that quote with another one, also from the *Catechism.*

"To understand this doctrine and practice of the Church ..." the *Catechism* says, "... it is necessary to understand that sin has *a double consequence"* [1472].

Every sin is two mess-ups in one!

"Grave sin deprives us of communion with God and therefore makes us incapable of eternal life, the privation of which is called the 'eternal punishment' of sin" [1472].

A "mortal" or deadly sin is our saying "no thanks" to God and his offer of heaven. Since he gives us free will, he *really* lets us choose him or reject him and he honors our decision. So, yes, there is a hell but it could be—as some saints have noted—empty.

"On the other hand every sin, even venial, entails an unhealthy attachment to creatures, which must be purified either here on earth, or after death, in the state called Purgatory" [1472].

Every sin, in some way or another, is our putting money, power, pleasure, toys—whatever—ahead of love of God and neighbor. Which isn't to say money, power, pleasure, toys and whatever are in themselves bad. It's that they can be, depending on how we use or abuse them. The famous quote "Money is the root of all evil" is a misquote. It's "the love of money" that is. "For the love of money is the root of all evils, and some people in their desire for it have strayed from the faith and have pierced themselves with many pains" (1 Timothy 6:10).

The *Catechism* continues: "This purification frees one from what is called the 'temporal punishment' of sin. These two punishments must not be conceived of as a kind of vengeance inflicted by God from without, but as following from the very nature of sin. A conversion which proceeds from a fervent charity can attain the complete purification of the sinner in such a way that no punishment would remain" [1472].[6] This means it's possible to go straight to heaven.

Original Sin and You

There's sin in the world now. There's no question about that. I sin, you sin, he and she sin. We sin, they sin. In big ways and in little ways, we choose evil over good.

But if God is all good (which is true), and everything created by God is good (which is true), why is there sin?

Part of the problem is our free will. We get to choose. I get to choose. I can do whatever I want with what God has created. For example, I can use my ability to speak to offer words of kindness or to skewer someone.

And part of it is original sin. "As a result of original sin," the *Catechism* says, "human nature is weakened in its powers; subject to ignorance, suffering and the domination of death; and inclined to sin. (This inclination is called 'concupiscence')" [418].

And, being human, we're hobbled with it from the get-go. It is "transmitted with human nature 'by propagation, not by imitation'" [419].

OK, but what *is* it?

"The account of the fall in *Genesis* 3," the *Catechism* says, "uses figurative language, but affirms a primeval event, a deed that took place *at the beginning of the history of man*....[7] The whole of human history is marked by the original fault freely committed by our first parents" [390].[8]

And, "After that first sin, the world is virtually inundated by sin" [401].

Here's what's important about original sin:

1. Our first parents sinned. They were encouraged by the devil, a fallen angel, who continues to encourage us to do the same.

2. The Gospels (the first four books of the New Testament) tell how God sent his Son to help get us back on track.

3. "The victory that Christ won over sin has given us greater blessings than those which sin had taken from us ..." [420]. We can have saints now—we can be saints now—because "where sin increased, grace abounded all the more" (the *Catechism* says, quoting Romans 5:20) [420].

The Garden of Eden was great, but what some have chosen because of Jesus, and what we can choose, is even greater.

Ask St. Joe:
Can There Be "Living" Saints?

Dear St. Joe:

I've heard some really outstanding people referred to as "living saints." Are they?

Wondering in Walla Walla

Dear Wondering:

Not technically. A really outstanding person can't be canonized while he or she is alive. The Church's formal process doesn't even begin until the person has died.

But that's not to say some folks who are alive today aren't going to be canonized in years to come. Every age and every generation seem to have some examples of a life led with heroic virtue. You might want to consider living your own that way. I highly recommend it.

St. Joe

Quote / Unquote

In that Mystical Body of Christ [that is, the Church with Jesus as its head], "thanks to the Communion of Saints, no good can be done, no virtue practiced by individual members, without its contributing something also to the salvation of all."

—Pope Pius XII

CHAPTER TWO

Canonization I: The Early Years

The Way We Were

It's tempting, comforting and incorrect to think that without exception the way the Church does things now is the way it has always done them. And that that method was firmly established by Jesus.

But that's not the case. There has been a development of doctrine over the centuries. Saints—or, rather, the making of saints—is a good example.

For instance: Peter, the first pope, canonized how many saints? None.

And he was canonized by ...? In a very real sense, by the community. It wasn't that they held a secret ballot. It was that they all knew how he died: killed for the faith.

You may have never cared for history in school, so I'll make this lesson very brief.

1. For the first three hundred years of Christianity, it was against the law to be a Christian.
2. The penalty for getting caught breaking this law was death.
3. Many folks broke this law and were caught.
4. They were put to death.

Unless a person has lived in a country where there is religious persecution (and, sadly, there still are places like that in our world), it's hard to imagine what those conditions are like. Those who have suffered persecution and those who still do know that the fanciful image many of us have of martyrdom falls far short of the brutal reality.

The early Christians knew the reality from the time of the apostles. After all, their leader—the Messiah, the "Anointed One"—had been arrested, tortured and executed. John the Baptist, who had announced his coming, had been imprisoned and beheaded.

In the Acts of the Apostles, the story of the first martyrdom is the stoning of Stephen (Acts 7:54-60). A deacon knocked to his knees in a hail of stones and bashed to death by a mob.

Those folks took off their cloaks and had a young fellow keep an eye on their stuff so nobody walked off with it. His name was Saul, later changed to Paul.

It was easy to recognize a saint in those early years. Only someone totally committed to Jesus would endure such things. Who would argue that Stephen *wasn't* worthy of being remembered? Worthy of being prayed to?

The decision was spontaneous. Complete. And right.

At that time, all who followed The Way—all those who were baptized in the name of the Father, Son and Holy Spirit—were considered "saints" or holy ones (*hagioi* in Greek). But some among them were called to be "witnesses"—martyrs in Greek.

Who opposed this little rag-tag band that claimed its leader had conquered death and gone to heaven, body and soul? Two very important groups. First, the local government—the Jewish officials who had seen more than their share of phony messiahs down through the years. And second, the Romans.

The first group wanted to keep a lid on Christianity because they were being watched and ruled over by the second group.

Palestine was an occupied territory. Its leaders had to keep its keepers happy.

The Roman Empire Strikes Back

A pip-squeak offshoot of Judaism—which was how early Christianity was viewed—was hardly a blip on the Roman radar screen, but Rome wanted no blips.

This meant that it wasn't just in their own homeland that the followers of Jesus were in danger, but throughout the empire. And the empire pretty much covered all the Mediterranean, Europe and western Asia. Rome was everywhere. And Rome had declared itself an enemy of Christianity. (Or more accurately, had declared Christianity its enemy.)

On the other hand, because Rome was the center of the known world, if your message became known there, it could spread to the farthest reaches of the empire's influence. And the story of Jesus, the Good News—the Gospel—of his coming to save humanity, did spread. Those pioneers in the faith prayed together, met for the breaking of the bread (the Mass) and were noticed by others. ("See how they love one another" is how the third-century theologian Tertullian put it.)

In spite of the dangers, it was attractive. But because of the dangers, membership wasn't automatic. A catechumen (one preparing for baptism) had to learn about The Way and had to realize this was a life-threatening decision. Catechumens spent years in the process. But even so, there were many who were anxious to join the Church.

Why? Well, obviously because then, as now, people can recognize the truth and, inspired by the Holy Spirit, can move in the direction in which God is calling them. But also—and the early Church believed this just as the Church today does—those who died for the faith, these witnesses, these saints, were a tremendous blessing that promoted the growth of the Church. Tertullian put it this way: "We multiply whenever we are mown down by you; the blood of Christians is seed."

Ignatius of Antioch

Early Christians knew from the start that there was the distinct possibility they would be killed. They accepted that. Some even looked forward to it and wanted to be sure their fellow believers didn't prevent it. The classic example is Ignatius, the second bishop of Antioch in Syria. Convicted of being a Christian, he was shipped to Rome, and all along the way fellow Christians went down to the docks to see him. He begged them not to interfere with his martyrdom. (Not that they could have.)

Rather, he said, "let me be eaten by the wild beasts, through whom I can reach the presence of God. I am God's wheat, and I am ground by the teeth of wild beasts so that I may be found pure bread of Christ."

That wild beast stuff was no exaggeration. During those first three hundred years, the risks for Christians varied from place to place and time to time. But some emperors were notorious for their creativity when it came to execution. It was well known that martyrdom was a spectator sport in the Eternal City. (*Go to: "An Afternoon's Entertainment."*)

That's where Ignatius died, killed by lions. A contemporary described what happened, noting that "only the harder portions of his holy remains were left." These, the writer said, "were [taken back] to Antioch, wrapped in linen, as an inestimable treasure left to the holy Church by the grace which was in the martyr."

Our Christian ancestors considered the scant remains left from martyrdom sacred relics. (We'll talk more about relics in chapter seven.) These "treasures" were treated with great respect, and the place where a "saint" was buried was considered holy. It was not unusual that, over time, a shrine built over that grave became a chapel. Then a church. And, finally, a basilica.

Spontaneously, a cult developed around these holy people. A particular devotion to them sprang up. (*Go to: "When Is a Cult Not a Cult?"*)

But it wasn't just those who actually died but those who were willing to face death who could be considered holy. These "confessors" admitted publicly they were followers of Christ despite the risk. Some were tortured and imprisoned but survived. Some of them also came to be called saints.

From the Hit List to the Hip List

The threat of martyrdom or of torture and imprisonment disappeared in A.D. 313 when the Emperor Constantine declared that Christianity was no longer outlawed. More than that, over time, the Church came to be the favorite of the upper crust. While, obviously, this was welcomed by Jesus' followers, it also presented some problems.

In the past, a person joined the Church because he or she really wanted to do that, despite the danger. Now some opted to be a part of it because membership was "in." And, needless to say, some weren't necessarily sincere in their commitment to what Christianity was all about.

And with regard to sainthood, how could there be saints who hadn't faced at least the possibility of martyrdom? How could the local community tell that someone who died of natural causes was really worthy of the kind of attention paid to a person who gave his or her life for Christ? Or gave his or her life just as Christ gave his?

Perhaps even more troubling personally, how could an individual imitate Christ if he or she wasn't likely to be killed for the faith? At a time when Christianity seemed to lose its edge and the possibility of a "soft" Christian or in-name-only believer became much more likely, some deliberately chose a harsh lifestyle. A pseudo-martyrdom to be lived day by day.

These were the hermits—surviving alone in caves or abandoned structures, living on food scraps and water, dedicating their whole being to prayer. Over time, some began to attract followers. Other men and women wanted to live near them and be like them. The fledgling communities of these "Desert Fathers"—struggling in Egypt and Syria—were the ancestors of today's monasteries and of the religious orders of men and women.

Also, over time, although these leaders had left the world, the world found them. They became well known as holy people. And when they died, again by spontaneous acclamation and action, they were named "saints." The stories of their lives were told. The words they had written were passed on. Their graves, and their relics, were deemed sacred. Just as people had come to see them, to seek their advice and to ask for their prayers when they were alive, now folks made pilgrimages to the places where they were buried.

Gradually, more categories of "saints" were included. Some brought the Good News to distant lands. Some were bishops. Some were royalty. Some were great defenders of the faith— "apologists"—who countered a variety of heresies. Some began religious orders. But all who were not "martyrs" continued to be called "confessors." And, not infrequently, it was more than how they had lived that brought them a following. It was miracles attributed to them, both before and after their deaths. (We'll examine that more closely in chapter six.)

No matter what kind of saint the person was, he or she was remembered by name when Christians came together to pray. At Mass, a list might be included. (And still is. The "canon" of the Mass—the Eucharistic prayer that includes the words of consecration—may feature the names of those early saints.)

In those early centuries, a local community might include a local saint in its "calendar." Remembering a hometown hero on his or her "feast day"—that is, the day of death (the day of entering heaven). Monasteries had their own calendars. So did some countries. (*Go to: "Pencil Me In: The Liturgical Calendar."*)

But, as we'll see in the next chapter, it wouldn't be until the end of the tenth century that the Church would have its first papal canonization.

An Afternoon's "Entertainment"

Obviously, grisly executions were not uncommon in the Roman Empire. The whipping and crucifixion of Jesus were not out of the ordinary. (On Good Friday, two other men were executed with Christ.)

Even so, during those early centuries when Christianity was outlawed, capital punishment moved from public deterrent to afternoon spectacle.

It was theater and sport. Audiences packed those vast arenas in Rome and elsewhere.

So now, many centuries later, it's important for us to remember, or to realize for the first time, that those men, women and children who were mauled and eaten by wild animals, pulled apart, burned, beheaded and hacked to pieces *were just like us.*

They had mothers and fathers. Brothers and sisters. They had husbands and wives. Sons and daughters. They feared pain. They feared death. They screamed and cried and lost control of their bodies as they met death.

But they took Jesus at his word and they displayed incredible faith and courage. Courage not being the absence of fear but, rather, staying faithful in spite of it.

And after it was over, after the crowd had left that arena, that circus, that coliseum (or *the* Colosseum), loved ones came forward and gathered the remnants. Like the friends of Ignatius of Antioch, they collected these "treasures" and treated them with untold respect and tenderness.

If we're going to understand those early martyrs, we have to get rid of our own romantic (and inaccurate) image of martyrdom. We have to see it for what it was. (And even in our own time, what it is.) So much more than a pious image on a holy card.

And we have to begin to appreciate how devastated and frightened and grief-stricken those early Christian communities were when one of their own—one of their beloved—was slaughtered. (Who would be next? Maybe me. And if it is, will I have enough faith to die as well?)

The stories of the deaths of the early martyrs were told over and over because their biographies offered more than inspiration, they offered a reminder: This could happen to any Christian.

Following Jesus was to be taken seriously because it was clearly a matter of life and death.

When Is a Cult Not a Cult?

It can be a little startling to read that an ancient local community developed a cult centered around a "local saint." In everyday conversation, "cult" means a pseudo-religious group with an unbalanced leader.

But it also refers to something else. It means the devotion or honor given to a person. Even in our own time, grassroots-level cults have developed. Two examples would be devotion to Salvadoran Archbishop Oscar Romero (killed in 1980 while saying Mass) and Mother Teresa of Calcutta.

As we'll see in chapter three, that type of cult is still something "saint makers" look for. The pope issues the final declaration concerning a saint but the process still begins locally. It's necessary to get the whole process started.

And as long as we're talking about devotion, here are three very technical words the Church uses:

—*Dulia* (from the Greek for "respect") means the kind and degree of honor given to angels and saints. (A thank-you prayer to St. Jude or lighting a candle in front of a statue of St. Thérèse is a form of dulia.)

—*Hyperdulia* (and we all know what "hyper" means) is above dulia. It's the praise given to Mary alone because, in all creation, she has a unique spot in the history of salvation. (Saying the rosary, or even a Hail Mary, is hyperdulia.)

—*Latria* (from the Greek for "service") is the kind and degree of praise reserved for God alone. (The ultimate form of latria is the Mass.)

Pencil Me In: The Liturgical Calendar

The Roman Catholic Church has a "calendar" that features a series of liturgical seasons (like Advent before Christmas and Lent before Easter) and commemorations of "divine mysteries" (like the Ascension), of Mary and of saints. A saint's feast day is superseded by a Sunday liturgy or what we might call a "bigger" feast.

But the Church's calendar isn't unchangeable. In fact, it was revised in 1969.

Some former feasts were dropped or relegated to particular places by local option because either there wasn't enough historical evidence for observing the feast worldwide or there wasn't "universal significance." This means a saint's feast isn't necessarily celebrated everywhere.

A good example would be St. Elizabeth Ann Seton, the first American-born saint. Her feast day would be celebrated in America because she's on the particular calendar for the United States. But parishes in Nigeria or New Zealand would have

Masses without prayers to her or about her. (*Go to: "Yankee Doodle Saints."*)

Here's another example: Say you were attending Mass at a parish run by Jesuits, and it was the feast day of some relatively obscure member of the society. It's likely that saint would be remembered there but not at the parish next door run by the Franciscans. And on a "Franciscan feast day," the opposite might happen.

That's not because of some big rivalry between the two. It just makes sense. Some countries, regions or groups are "closer" to a particular saint. They want to honor him or her on that day. (Folks in Brooklyn aren't likely to have a special Mass remembering some saint who is the patron of a village in Bavaria.)

Put it in very ordinary terms. Suppose your mother and a friend's father happen to have the same birthday. Whose name are you going to put on the cake at your house?

Of course.

Now, suppose your friend's mother's birthday is today. They're having a cake at their place but you're having an ordinary dinner at yours.

For many people, that's what a particular devotion is like. (We'll discuss that more in chapter eight.) A saint, for whatever reason, has become a friend. (A companion, a mentor, a confidant, an inspiration, a helper.) Folks in one town love her. Members of one order call on him often.

What's really amazing and possible for anyone including you or me is that that same kind of relationship can be established between an individual and a saint. You can become friends with the biggest names in Church history (or the most modest). How? The same as becoming friends with anyone. Spend time talking (that is, praying). And get to know him or her better. (Read up on that person and check out what he or she has written.) The Communion of Saints makes this possible.

The feasts of some saints are celebrated worldwide. But most will be remembered only locally. And those who are one step away from canonization—the "blessed"—are remembered locally. (We'll take a look at the "blesseds" in chapter three.) The Church says they can be honored and prayed to publicly, but they aren't yet canonized. They aren't yet on the universal calendar.

Yankee Doodle Saints

Celebrations on the particular calendar for the U.S. include:

January 4: Elizabeth Ann Seton

January 5: John Neumann

January 6: Blessed André Bessette

March 3: Katharine Drexel

May 15: Isidore the Farmer

July 1: Blessed Junípero Serra

July 4: Independence Day (a special Mass for the United States)

July 14: Blessed Kateri Tekakwitha

August 18: Jane Frances de Chantal

September 9: Peter Claver

October 6: Blessed Marie Rose Durocher

October 19: Isaac Jogues, John de Brebeuf and Companions

October 20: Paul of the Cross

November 13: Frances Xavier Cabrini

November 18: Rose Philippine Duchesne

November 23: Blessed Miguel Agustin Pro

Fourth Thursday of November: Thanksgiving Day (another United States Mass)

December 9: Blessed Juan Diego

December 12: Our Lady of Guadalupe

Ask St. Joe:
What's With Those Swallows?

Dear St. Joe:

When do the swallows come back to Capistrano?

Budding Birder

Dear Birder:

Not to be immodest but tradition says these feathered friends return to San Juan Capistrano Mission (in the California town with the same name) on my feast day, March 19.

They aren't always punctual. But close. (It depends on the weather and food supply.)

And by the way, speaking of Church calendars, it's a general law of the Church that my feast day is a holy day of obligation. But it's not observed that way in the Church in the United States.

St. Joe

Quote / Unquote

"The martyrs were bound, imprisoned, scourged, racked, burnt, rent, butchered—and they multiplied."

—St. Augustine (354–430)

CHAPTER THREE

Canonization II:
Those Marvelous Middle Ages

Distinguishing the Very Good
From the Very, Very Good

During the early centuries of the Church, every saint was—in one way or another—a hometown hero or heroine. But then, just about any community at just about any point in time has somebody who's very good. Very holy. Very saintly.

So if, during those ancient Church times, that person *didn't* die for the faith, if that person was a "non-martyr," how were locals supposed to *really* tell if the recently deceased was a saint or just a good person? It would take a miracle.

That was the clincher. It was one promoted by Church leaders, including the very influential Augustine, a fourth-century bishop, theologian and writer. (And saint and Doctor—great teacher—of the Church.) In his *City of God*, he included examples of miracles attributed to saints.

At that time, folks in the Holy Land claimed they had discovered the body of St. Stephen (the deacon who was the Church's first martyr). His remains were distributed to various shrines in various countries. There were claims of cures at these spots after the relics arrived. (We'll look more closely at relics in chapter seven.)

Augustine thought they were genuine miracles. So did a lot of people. That was why the recipe for saint making began to include four mandatory ingredients. (Ingredients that would later become the official process.)

To make a saint, one needed a person who:

1. Was dead.
2. Had a "cult" or a reputation among the people. (A *good* reputation, obviously.)
3. Had stories told about him or her that showed this individual had "heroic virtue."
4. Was known for producing miracles. In particular after his or her death at shrines or through the person's relics.

At that time, understandably, the criteria for judging miracles was extremely simple, especially compared with what it is today. Back then no one called for a thorough investigation of the miraculous. And while there were folks who discredited some claims, it would be a few hundred more years before the Church would insist on examinations to make sure what the locals reported was accurate.

Enter the Bishops and Popes

But for quite a while the details weren't all that important. It was the cult—the public devotion—that mattered. A saint was someone who was remembered and honored and prayed to.

From the years 500 to 900 the number of saints mushroomed. As countries in northern and eastern Europe were introduced to Christianity, folks there wanted and spotted their "own" saints. The Church thought that was a good idea and it encouraged the veneration of relics. In fact, the use and misuse of relics greatly shaped the canonization process.

Now getting someone declared a saint became a bit more complicated but not overwhelmingly difficult.

Bishops' roles became more prominent because bishops were in charge of overseeing the shrines housing relics. If a shrine is in my diocese—within the boundaries of that geographic area—then I'm responsible for what's happening there. I want to know what's going on and I want to make sure all those goings-on are on the up and up. (*Go to: "The Making of a Medieval Saint."*)

In the process that developed, the bishop gave the OK for a person's body to be dug up and transferred to an altar. This "translation" became the sign that he or she was officially canonized and that name was added to the local calendar of saints.

Bishops were no fools. They started to realize it wasn't just a reputation that made a saint. Somebody needed to really check out the facts behind the legends. By the end of the tenth century, some people thought that the Holy Father was just the person for the job. Not only would the burden be on the pontiff then, but if he gave his approval, that local saint would have an even bigger name.

Historians say that was why Pope John XV approved the canonization of Bishop Ulrich of Augsburg in 993. He heard the reports about the holy man's life and miracles and authorized the translation of the body.

The canonization process continued to develop over the next seven hundred years. And the role, function and power of the papacy needed some sorting out, too.

What was the problem? The problem was local folk—meaning the immediate community and its bishop—had been saying who was and who wasn't a saint and then, over time, they were expected to hand over the reins to Rome.

Look, the locals explained, that idea may fly in ... Florence or Naples or some other burg on the Italian peninsula (and it may not), but that's not how we do things in Munich. Or Paris. Or London.

And—here's another touchy point—what about "our" saints that Rome might not necessarily approve of? Is the pope now going to say the patron of some town or region (*our* town or region) *isn't* a saint?

Or from the point of view of some people in Rome—why should some monk in the heart of "Nowhereville" be considered a saint just because the locals say so? Or because they said so a hundred or two hundred or five hundred years ago?

But, surely, politics and pettiness wouldn't influence members of the Roman Catholic Church. Well ... (*Go to: "Church Politics and Infallibility."*)

Less People and More Papal

Two popes came along who helped solve the problems. The first was Alexander III (1159–1181). He wasn't just a pope. He was a lawyer. He figured some order—some rules—were needed. And he figured he was just the fellow to write and enforce them. (Not just when it came to making saints. When it came to a lot of things.)

In 1170, Alexander decreed nobody—*nobody*—was going to be venerated locally without a papal say-so. The Late, Great Abbot So-and-So may truly be worthy of a public cult but he wasn't getting it until Alexander allowed it.

That was the theory. Some bishops continued to canonize.

Some communities continued to established cults.

Enter Gregory IX. In 1234, he published his "Decretals"—a collection of papal laws. In black and white, in a binding law that applied to the universal Church, he said absolute jurisdiction over the causes of saints was the pope's.

He reasoned that a saint is the object of devotion for the whole Church. So only the pope—the bishop with universal jurisdiction—has the authority to declare someone a saint. More rules were needed because a saint's cause always began at the local level. Without that, few cases would end up in Rome. So local tribunals were created. Their delegates would present the pontiff with testimony from witnesses backing the candidate's virtue. And his or her miracles.

However, the Vatican was serious about the no-new-cults rule. It banned the publication of books on the miracles or private revelations of local saints and even said images of these people couldn't include halos and such.

Court Is Now in Session

But saying the Vatican was serious is a bit of a misstatement. We have to remember that canonization wasn't the only item on the papal plate. And, as a matter of fact, the papal plate wasn't even at the Vatican for a while. From 1309 to 1377 the Church was run from Avignon, France, after Clement V decided to abandon Rome.

It was at Avignon that even more canonical (legal) reforms took place. Among them, the canonization process became a "trial."

There were:

—The "petitioners" who wanted to get someone canonized.

—Their official "procurator" or "prosecutor" of the cause who pushed the petitioners' case. (Here prosecutor doesn't mean the one trying to prove wrongdoing.)

—The pope, represented by a newly created position, "the promoter of the faith." Over time, this job acquired the common title "the devil's advocate." It wasn't that this official was cooperating with Satan, but he was the stickler who made sure this so-called saint was *really* a saint.

The process also demanded letters from monarchs and others saying that they wanted this to happen. It wasn't going to fly at all if only the little folks backed the deceased.

A trial could last for months and was held locally. Hundreds of witnesses could be called on to testify, and the recent flood of saints was squeezed to a trickle. From 1200 to 1334 there were only twenty-six papal canonizations.

Rome may have spoken, but that didn't shut up the people. That trial stuff was all well and good but this holy man, this holy woman, is *the town's patron.*

Devotions to local saints blossomed and new cults formed. They were also springing up in some newly formed "mendicant" (beggar) orders. (The Franciscans and the Dominicans are "mendicants.")

Well, said Rome, then these men and women, who may indeed have shown heroic virtue but who have not been officially canonized, are not "saints" but they are "blesseds." And a "blessed" can be venerated only locally or by a religious order. That's the way it will be until these "Servants of God," those somewhere along in the process, are officially canonized.

Which may or may not happen.

That distinction was lost, or ignored, by some locals. Their attitude seemed to be "You can call her one of the 'beati'—the 'blesseds'—but *we* know she's a saint!"

And once a saint is canonized, he or she can't be "downgraded" to some sort of "non-saint." What about St. Christopher? *Go to: "Mr. Christopher and the Jumble Saint."*

Now, before this happened, the list of saints was a pretty diverse group. Yes, they were all holy but they were clergy and laity, men and women, movers-and-shakers and "little people."

As the Vatican gained control of the process, fewer "little people" were introduced into the system. Rome had particular interest in some cases, and religious orders had the ability to work their own through all those ecclesiastical ins and outs.

This isn't to say those who were canonized didn't deserve to be. It's just that they were the squeakier wheels or it was prudent to see to it that some cases kept moving right along.

Even in our own time, it could be said without disrespect that Pope John Paul II's motto might have read: "Beatification, don't leave home without it." Many of his visits outside Italy included the beatification of local "Servants of God."

Can I Get an "Amen" From the Congregation?

As the years rolled by, "beatification" became an official step in the process, and in 1588 Pope Sixtus V created the Sacred Congregation of Rites. (A rite is a religious custom, usage or ceremony. Or it can be, one might say, a "branch" of the Church. We'll look at that in chapter four.) It was given the authority to oversee the process of canonization and to authenticate relics of the saints. (Pope Paul VI renamed it the Congregation for the Causes of Saints in 1969.) But it wasn't until the seventeenth century that Pope Urban VIII came up with specific rules for beatification and canonization.

Urban decreed any form of public veneration of an individual was forbidden until that person was beatified or canonized by papal declaration. Which brought up an interesting point.

If only the pope could do this, what about all the saints who had been declared saints before this without the pope's approval? Urban ruled if it could be shown a saint had a cult "from time immemorial" or that devotion to him or her could be justified "on the strength of what the Fathers [of the Church—the early theologians] or saints have written, with the ancient and conscious acquiescence of the Apostolic See or local bishops," then that was OK.

So now a saint was a saint if Rome canonized him or her, or if that person had a cult that was already at least a century old at the time of Urban's ruling. That "grandfather clause" made it easier for locals to accept the other decision about new names. But Urban stressed that from now on, if there was any unauthorized public cult for a person before he or she was beatified or canonized, that person was automatically disqualified from the process.

Locals could gather at that person's tomb and pray for help, including miracles. And they could meet in homes for private devotions, too. But there would be no veneration or praying to the person in a church.

Over the next century, canon lawyers (a canon lawyer is somebody trained in the laws of the Church) refined the rules of the game. Then one canon lawyer, who had become Pope Benedict XIV, gave himself the assignment of reviewing and clarifying the theory behind canonization and the method the Church was using.

The five volumes of his "On the Beatification of Servants of God and the Canonization of Blesseds" (*"De Servorum Dei beatificatione et Beatorum canonizatione"*) were published between 1734 and 1738.

It's still "it" when it comes to making saints. There would be other developments but the next benchmark wouldn't come until the twentieth century.

The Making of a Medieval Saint

From the fifth to the tenth centuries, bishops were the ones who called a lot of the shots when it came to making saints. They were the ones shaping the development of new cults.

What folks wanted was their choice added to the local calendar. But the bishops wouldn't give their OK before the "petitioner" handed over a written report on the holy one's life, virtues and death. These were called "vitae." (Latin for "life.") There also had to be accounts of any miracles and, if it applied, the particulars of his or her martyrdom.

Some sticklers also insisted on testimony from eyewitnesses, especially concerning any claims of miracles.

Most vitae were what we today would consider sugar-sweet accounts, and they were heavily laced with pious legends. A pious legend doesn't necessarily mean a fairy tale.

It's an account that can be accepted as true but one that may have been embellished over time. And not infrequently, "eyewitness" testimony was what someone said someone said someone said someone else saw.

This doesn't mean the dearly departed really *weren't* saints. It's just that some enthusiastic supporters crossed the line between telling the story and storytelling.

Once the bishop had given his nod (or a regional synod—a collections of bishops—approved), the person's body was exhumed and moved to an altar. This act came to symbolize canonization.

Then the new saint was given a day on the local calendar.

Church Politics and Infallibility

It's always tempting to have the misguided notion that at some point in history the Church ran smoothly from top to bottom, with no one (at best) making mistakes or (at worst) sinning big-time.

But the Church was and is made up of human beings who make mistakes and sin. They get stupid; they get greedy; they get lazy. They get mad and decide to get even.

For two thousand years we have been a collection of saints and scoundrels. At different points in our own lives, most of us have worn or come close to wearing both those hats.

It shouldn't be surprising that some Christian—a king, a pope, a whatever—messed up. While that can be disappointing, it does *not* mean:

1. The Church is filled with hypocrites and, therefore, is worthless.
2. The Church is going to fizzle out and die.

Yes, the Church has hypocrites. At times, each of us can be hypocritical. But—and this is important—the Church wasn't made for saints. The Church was made to make saints. To help us become saints. To help us reach heaven.

And arriving there is the basic definition of sainthood.

Yes, the Church as an institution, not as the People of God, is going to end. At the end of time, there will be no need for an institutional Church. But between now and then, it will continue to be guided by the Holy Spirit. As some folks have pointed out, if the Church weren't led by the Holy Spirit, it would have collapsed centuries ago.

Like proof?

Consider the apostles. The twelve leaders Jesus chose to begin his Church. His *handpicked* inner circle. Of those twelve, one ratted him out: Judas. And another, when the chips were down, publicly denied him three times: Peter.

And it was the denier who was supposed to lead the leaders. It was the denier, ashamed of his acts but not trying some cover-up or spin control, who *did* end up leading them. Did end up proclaiming the Good News despite the dangers it brought him. Did end up dying for Jesus and like Jesus. What happened? The Holy Spirit. Pentecost (Acts, chapter 2).

But wait a minute. If everyone can mess up, what is the deal with "papal infallibility"? Maybe we should begin with what that *doesn't* mean:

—A pope can't make a mistake.
—A pope can't sin.
—If a pope says it's going to rain, take your umbrella.

—If a pope puts twenty bucks on the Cubs, there are going to be a lot of happy people at Wrigley Field.

It means none of that.

Here's what the bishops at Vatican II said, in their Dogmatic Constitution on the Church:

"This infallibility with which the divine Redeemer willed his Church to be endowed in defining a doctrine of faith and morals extends as far as extends the deposit of divine revelation which must be religiously guarded and faithfully expounded.

"This is the infallibility which the Roman Pontiff ... enjoys in virtue of his office, when, as the supreme shepherd and teacher of all the faithful who confirms his brethren in their faith, he proclaims by a definitive act some doctrine of faith and morals."

That's it in a nutshell. A rather large nutshell.

More simply put: Jesus said the Church can define teaching when it comes to faith and morals. The pope is the head teacher. As such, he has the power and authority to make those decisions and when he does he can't be wrong.

This is known as the pope speaking *ex cathedra*—Latin for "from the chair" of St. Peter's—and it's done very rarely.

Mr. Christopher and the Jumble Saint

Many folks are under the false impression that St. Christopher was demoted.

A pious legend says Christopher made his living carrying people across a river. One day a child asked to be taken so Christopher put him on his shoulders and headed out. As they crossed, the boy got heavier and heavier. He then told Christopher he was Jesus. In fact, the name Christopher means "Christ bearer."

The patron of travelers, Christopher, who died around 251, has long been popular. Medals with his image are still big sellers. And recently, oddly enough, they've been made with sports themes: St. Christopher and soccer, St. Christopher and volleyball. And so on.

When a Vatican commission revised the General or Universal Calendar in 1969, Christopher's feast day, July 25, became optional and local. His disappearance was mistaken by some to mean he had been banished.

The case of St. Philomena is a little more complicated. Some Church historians say she was never canonized. Others claim she was. Philomena was thought to be a virgin martyr of the early Church whose remains were discovered in a Roman catacomb in 1802. The tomb had three stones with the inscription: LUMENA PAX TE CUM FI. When put in a particular order, they read "Pax tecum Filumena" ("Peace be with you, Filumena.") It was assumed she was a martyr and was venerated as such after miracles were reported at the translation of her relics.

In 1855, Pope Pius IX gave Philomena a Mass and she gained popularity. However, archaeologists have raised some doubts about the connection between the bones and the inscription. It was likely the two weren't related. So her public cult was suppressed by Pope John XXIII in 1961. That meant there could be no Masses or dedication of churches in her honor. Those already named for her were to be rededicated to someone else. They could, of course, be named for the *other* Philomena. That saint, whose feast day is July 5, died around 500.

Ask St. Joe

Dear St. Joe:

What do you think about this joke?

The Holy Family is having a barbecue in the backyard and you tip over the grill. Jesus turns to Mary and says, "Well, we can't all be perfect."

Catholic Comedian

Dear Comedian:

For your penance I want you to memorize every word I was credited with saying in all four Gospels.

St. Joe

P.S. It won't take you long. The evangelists didn't give me a single line!

Quote / Unquote

"How can we say that the Church wishes to bring us back to the Dark Ages? The Church was the only thing that ever brought us out of them."

—G.K. Chesterton (1874–1936)

CHAPTER FOUR

Canonization III:
Not Quite Thoroughly Modern

Under Four-Hundred-Year Warranty

By the early twentieth century, most folks—including Catholics—knew little of the inner workings of the canonization process. Even now, in the early twenty-first century, most folks—including Catholics—know little of the inner workings of the canonization process.

This doesn't mean there was some big conspiracy from the time of the Council of Trent in the sixteenth century or that Benedict XIV's lengthy work on beatification and canonization was Top Secret.

No, it was just that *"De Servorum Dei beatificatione et Beatorum canonizatione"* was in Latin. And few people one hundred years ago or last year were fluent in Latin or well-versed in canon law. *(Go to: "Decoding Canon Law.")*

In 1917 the process was made a part of it. But seven years earlier a book on the whole procedure had come out in English. Written by a British priest, it tended to be as lofty as the then very popular "lives of the saints" that dripped with amazing (some would say incredible) tales of men and women who were so good none of us could ever hope to come close to matching them.

But the clerics running the system knew they were examining the lives of mere mortals. Potential saints, yes, but mere mortals. Their investigations included a series of questions. They wanted to know if the candidate had a reputation for "heroic virtue" or had died as a martyr. Were people asking the candidate for help now? (The old spontaneous response from the people.) How would this canonization help the Church? Was there something in the candidate's life or writing that would stand in the way of canonization? Had there been claims of miracles? Was there any reason—any reason—the process shouldn't continue?

(With so much red tape and scrutinizing, it might seem there was no way a candidate could make it through the process. And certainly none who could do it quickly. But that wasn't true. One of the twentieth century's favorite saints pretty much sailed through. The case of St. Thérèse of Lisieux, the Little Flower, zipped along at break-neck speed. (*Go to: "The Little Way of St. Thérèse of Lisieux."*))

As always, the process was set up to begin in the local church or local diocese. There, under the guidance of the bishop, it was determined if the person:

1) had a reputation for holiness

2) deserved it.

While that was being looked into, everything—*everything*—that could be found which the person had written was sent to Rome to be checked for orthodoxy. A fellow might have been known as devout and an inspiration to all, but if he had penned a few letters to his brother saying, "I think this whole idea of the Trinity is a bunch of hokum," or, "I know God doesn't *really* exist but ..." then that was the end of that.

It seems safe to speculate most cases wouldn't be that black and white. It was those gray areas to which Rome took a magnifying glass.

After the local bishop handed the case over to Rome—sent all the material and testimony from that initial investigation—then it went to a Vatican consultor who picked out a defense lawyer for it. He—the lawyer—would present a brief (a legal document) defending the cause. That was countered by the promoter of the faith—the "devil's advocate."

This could take years. Once all the wrinkles were ironed out, once everyone had come to an agreement, the material was published in a volume known as the "positio." (What we might call the case file.)

The congregation's cardinals and other officials would study the positio and rule on it. If the decision was thumbs up, the congregation let the pope know and he could go on to accept it.

So then the person was canonized?

Oh, no. Not yet.

Step Two

Then came the "apostolic process." Now it was the Holy See's turn to check it *all* out. The cause went back to the local diocese and was looked at even more closely. Once it made it back to Rome, the defense lawyer and promoter of the faith had at it again. If the cause was given another green light, the candidate, or Servant of God, was given the title "Venerable."

(One change popped up after 1917; Pope Pius XI decided that the process needed a historical section. In 1930 he set up a method to handle ancient cases and lingering problems that needed special attention. In some instances, there were no eyewitnesses—they had all died centuries earlier. In others, there was a need for historical research. Then, too, it could be necessary to have the origin, existence and continuation of a cult looked at. Some of those devotions would have had a following that dated back further than papal canonizations. More than three hundred individuals have had their cults confirmed in this way. In those instances, the pope can make a decree of "equivalent" beatification or canonization.)

It was at this point that the person's corpse was examined. (*Go to: "When Your Great-Uncle Is on the Saint-Track."*) The local bishop coordinated this. One reason for the look-see was to make sure it was the right body. If locals were flocking to a gravesite that wasn't the venerable's, well ... that wasn't good at all. Then prayers and devotions had to stop because they were praying and offering devotions at the wrong spot.

Then, too, it could be considered a plus if the venerable's body wasn't corrupt. An unofficial plus. If the body had naturally decayed, that wasn't necessarily a minus. The Roman Catholic Church doesn't say an uncorrupted body is a sign of holiness. Church officials know there could be natural reasons for this.

It wasn't that way in centuries past. Then it was thought a saint's corpse had a sweet scent—known as the "odor of sanctity." If one was still in (relatively) good condition, that was taken as a sign the person truly had been holy.

(Many European churches boast the corpse of a saint in a glass coffin. Natives say he or she is as handsome or lovely as ever. Tourists—even sincere pilgrims—might disagree.)

At this point the body could be moved to a location—a shrine, a church, a chapel, a cemetery—which was better able to accommodate visitors, or easier to get to.

Out of Rome's Hands

This was where the process shifted gears. The next step, it might be said, was up to God. Fallible humans had overseen things but now the operation would sputter—stall but not die—unless and until there was a divine sign that this person should be declared a saint.

Well, a couple of divine signs. The process had required two miracles for a beatification. For nonmartyrs. And two more for canonization. (We really will look at miracles in chapter six.) In more recent years, that regulation has loosened up some, but it's still a tough one.

After that miraculous intervention, but before beatification, the cardinals of the congregation got together again with the pope to see if the next step should be taken. More than a mere formality, it could halt the procedure. A pope could decide "not now" and the venerable would be shelved. Or he could give his OK and issue a decree announcing his decision.

At the beatification ceremony, the pope proclaimed that this person was to be venerated as one of the Church's "blesseds." But only in a local diocese, region (which could be a country) or among members of a particular religious order. The Holy See authorized a special prayer to the blessed and Mass in his or her honor.

Traditionally, many beatifications have been held at St. Peter's in Rome but they don't have to be. John Paul II is famous for hosting the ceremony during a visit to the country of the man or woman of the hour.

There's no guarantee a "blessed" will ever become a saint. From the Church's point of view, again, that's up to God. It takes a miracle for canonization. A blessed may stay in that "on-deck circle" for centuries. Possibly until the end of time.

There are hundreds of blesseds in the Congregation for the Causes of Saints' active file, including some—at the beginning of the twenty-first century—who are well known and loved in the United States. (*Go to: "North America's Blesseds."*)

Once miracles have been attributed, examined and verified, the pope issues a "bull" of canonization. (A most unfortunate word, considering modern slang, but a "bull" is an official papal document.) It says the person must be venerated throughout the Church. In ceremonies at St. Peter's, the pope demonstrates the new saint has his complete approval. During the liturgy, the pontiff describes the life of the saint and explains how his or her example and message apply today.

New and Improved

While many observers have noticed John Paul II is a saint-maker like no other pontiff, few have realized that one reason he has been able to beatify and canonize so many people is because of changes in the procedure.

During Vatican II, under Pope Paul VI, a commission started taking a long hard look at the method the Church was using. John Paul II finished the reorganization in 1983.

Under the new method, evidence is gathered locally and doesn't require the apostolic process. (That double-checking of everything by Rome.) And the "trial" approach was changed to one of research. The lengthy (and time-consuming) arguments between the defense lawyer and the promoter of the faith were tossed. So, in a sense, was the promoter of the faith, the old "devil's advocate." That job title was changed to "prelate theologian."

In the next chapter, we'll see how, using the new method, you could get a friend canonized.

Decoding of Canon Law

What's a "canon"?

"Canon" comes from the Greek word *kanon* which means a rule or standard. It's also a list. ("Cannon" is the gun.)

So is the Code of Canon Law some secret list or set of laws that needs to be "decoded"?

No. The Code of Canon Law is a collection of the universal and fundamental laws of the Roman Catholic Church.

If it's not a secret, how come I've never seen a copy of it?

Have you looked? Copies are available to anyone through any major bookseller.

Where did it come from?

From the time of the apostles, Church leaders got together and made common decisions about how things should be done. Later, as membership grew and spread out, there were local and regional meetings—"synods"— as well as general councils, when all leaders tried to get together.

Since those early times, those decisions were often written in brief statements that came to be called canons. In those early years there was little effort made to collect all of them or put them in any order.

Why not?

For the first three centuries, Christians had bigger fish

to fry. Like staying alive, because of religious persecution.

Numbers skyrocketed in the fourth century and new laws were needed. People wanted to know what the Church taught and how they were supposed to act. For example, laws covered how clergy and married folks were supposed to behave and the nuts-and-bolts of Church activity.

Over time, the lists were collected and compiled. And then the collections were sorted out and canon law itself became a discipline (an area of study).

So this is all ancient history?

Not really. The final decision to codify the material—to put all the laws in order—was made by Pope Pius X in 1903. The Code of Canon Law, the first official guide to the laws of the Catholic Church, came out in 1917. It was revised in 1965 and 1982, and that revision was published in 1983.

The current code has 1,752 individual canons divided into seven books. They deal with various aspects of Church life and organization.

The Little Way of St. Thérèse of Lisieux

Under the canonization process prior to 1917, Thérèse of Lisieux wouldn't have even been eligible for consideration until fifty years after her death—meaning 1947. But that was the old system. Her cause had already been introduced, examined and approved by 1925. That year she was added to the Church's calendar.

Born in 1873 in Alençon, France, Thérèse made her vows at the Carmelite convent at Lisieux in 1890. Her older sister—biological sister—was the superior there. (There were five girls in the Martin family. All became nuns. Four of them Carmelites. Thérèse was the baby.)

Her sister ordered her to write about her childhood and then she was asked to write about her life in the convent. So, although she lived in obscurity and died of tuberculosis at the age of twenty-four, her autobiography—the telling of her mystical experiences—became known worldwide after her death. *The Story of a Soul* described Thérèse's "little way" to holiness.

The point she stressed was anyone could reach sainthood anywhere. With God's help, of course.

And Thérèse really wanted to be a saint.

(The book makes for interesting reading. Some readers especially enjoy the part when Thérèse admits there was at least one other community member who drove her right up the wall.)

In 1997, she was named a Doctor of the Church. That's an honor that has been given to thirty-three saints. And only three of them female.

The fifty-year rule is off the books but it's still considered a wise guideline. There will be exceptions, of course, but it seems the Church wants to keep those cases ... exceptional.

Why the delay? Common sense, really. The saintmakers want to be sure a person's reputation for virtue isn't just media hype. If it's authentic, the reasoning goes, people will still be drawn to this person half a century later. And any private following or devotion that sprung up soon after his or her death will still be going strong.

When Your Great-Uncle Is on the Saint-Track

A very recent—in Church terms—example of a "translation" is Father Solanus Casey.

Born near Oak Grove, Wisconsin, in 1870, Barney Casey entered the Capuchin Order at the age of twenty-six. Considered a marginal student by his superiors, "Father Solanus" was ordained a "simplex priest" and allowed to say Mass but not to preach formal sermons or hear confessions. (Attending a seminary where classes were taught in German had made those school years even harder for the English-speaking student.)

Assigned as a doorkeeper, he went on to counsel and pray with thousands who came to see this humble monk who, many believe, was a wonder-worker dispensing God's mercy and healing. Father Solanus died in 1957.

Because he was one of fourteen living siblings (two others died when they were children), he had scores of nieces, nephews, grandnieces and grandnephews.

Two of them were on hand when the priest's body was exhumed in 1987. While not serving in any official capacity during the ceremony, they represented the family. Sister Anne Herkenrath, the granddaughter of Father Solanus' oldest brother James, talked about her great-uncle.

Did you know Father Solanus when you were a child?

I did. I had the opportunity to meet him on two occasions. He came [from Detroit] to our home on Lake Washington [in Seattle] for a family gathering in 1945, to attend the first Mass of a nephew, Jesuit Father John McCluskey. This was a big event for the family. Father Solanus was with us for the day. He was like all the other uncles, just one of the family doing family things. He loved riding in the boat, visiting, playing the violin and singing on a home recording. He even played a little baseball. As a young man he had been the catcher for the "Casey Nine," the all-brothers' team.

What were your impressions of him?

As an active teenager, I was thrilled to get to know him in such an ordinary way. He was just a very wonderful, normal human being. Very loving, peaceful, joyous with a good sense of humor—always a twinkle in his eye. He was fun.

Growing up, we were in awe of him. We had been hearing stories of remarkable things happening as a result of Solanus' prayers, but we in the family were encouraged to be silent. Father Solanus' brother, Msgr. Edward Casey, said that these stories were not something the family should get involved with. This was between Solanus and God and his Capuchin brothers. In other words, talk of holiness was not a thing to be exploited.

He would write letters, especially to my grandparents, and send us mementos or holy cards for special events such as First Communion. We knew who he was and we knew he was a very holy man but didn't pay a lot of attention to what he did.

After his death family members began to be asked many questions. It was then that we started to get into his story.

You met him a second time after the day on the lake?

In 1948, when I was in the Midwest, I had the opportunity to go with an aunt and two young cousins to visit him at the monastery in Huntington, Indiana. This was a busy time for him; and he didn't have a lot of time to spend with us but we had a very enjoyable dinner and breakfast the next day with him.

At that time in my life I was thinking about becoming a religious. It was a time of struggle for me and I found reasons to hesitate. While at the monastery I thought since Father Solanus was so holy and knew these things I would just ask him. So, I did. He looked at me and said, "That is between you and God. You have to do this yourself."

Well, I was disappointed. I was actually kind of mad at him. I wanted him to say "no" but he wouldn't tell me what to do.

What happened at the "translation"?

When I went back to Detroit in 1987, I was one of two family members present for the process. We were not official. My cousin, Dr. Michael Casey, is a dentist and was there in case additional identification was needed. This was not necessary because Solanus was very recognizable. There was no hesitation about who this man was.

The pathologist, several other medical personnel and Church dignitaries including Archbishop Szoka of Detroit were present.

Solanus had been buried in the Capuchian cemetery there. His coffin was dug up and wheeled into the monastery chapel's sacristy.

When they opened the casket they found the lining and much of his clothing in shreds. But he was very serene. His forearms and hands were bones but the rest of his body was fairly intact. His beard was scraggly (as it was when he died, because at the time of his death in the hospital, one of my relatives who was one of his nurses had snipped clippings from his beard).

Then what happened?

Then they clothed him in a new habit. Before placing him in the new casket everyone broke for lunch but I remained in that quiet place with him for nearly an hour. It was a powerful, prayerful time for me.

That day was an awesome event—a beautiful moment in my life and I believe in the life of the Church. I truly believe that this is a man who will be canonized someday.

Father Solanus Casey was declared "venerable" in July of 1995. It is said that this step is the hardest part—to prove that he lived a life of heroic virtue.

So who knows what will happen or when? But his work goes on. Many people in many countries all over the world know about him and pray to him quite earnestly.

North America's Blesseds

You may have noticed the list of "U.S. feasts" in chapter three contained a number of blesseds. Here's a brief run-down of who's who (although between the time this book is published and you read it, some may have already been canonized).

Blessed André Bessette (1845–1937) was a Canadian Holy Cross brother and the driving force behind the building of St. Joseph's Oratory in Montreal. It's said some one million people came to pay their respects during the public viewing before his funeral. He was beatified in 1982, and his feast day is January 6.

Blessed Junípero Serra (1713–1784) was a Spanish Franciscan priest who established nine of the twenty-one Franciscan missions along the Pacific coast. One of California's two representatives in Statuary Hall in Washington, D.C., he was beatified in 1988. His feast day is July 1.

Blessed Kateri Tekakwitha (1656–1680) is known as the "Lily of the Mohawks." Born in what is now Auriesville, New York, she lived a life devoted to prayer and penance and took care of the sick and elderly. She was beatified in 1980, and her feast day is July 14.

Blessed Marie Rose Durocher (1811–1849)—and, yes, baseball great Leo was in the same family tree—was a Canadian who began the Sisters of the Holy Names of Jesus and Mary. She was beatified in 1984. Her feast day is October 6.

Blessed Miguel Agustin Pro (1891–1927) was a Mexican Jesuit priest unjustly accused of taking part in a plot to kill the Mexican president. He was arrested and executed. He was beatified in 1988, and his feast day is November 23.

Blessed Juan Diego (sixteenth century) was a Mexican Indian to whom Our Lady of Guadalupe appeared. He was beatified in 1990, and his feast day is December 9.

Ask St. Joe:
How Many of Us Are There?

Dear St. Joe:

How many saints share your—our—name? Was there ever a Pope Joseph?

A Fellow Joseph

Dear Fellow:

There are quite a few "Holy Joes." One recent book of saints listed thirty-three. As for a pontiff, no. And there probably never will be. It has become the custom for popes to take the name of a predecessor. Or—in the case of the two recent John Pauls—a combination of predecessors. Since there never was a Joseph, odds are there never will be. (There's been only one Peter, but then that apostle was one of a kind!)

St. Joe

Quote / Unquote

"No devotion to the saints is more acceptable and more proper than if you strive to express their virtues."

—Erasmus (1466–1536), Dutch scholar

CHAPTER FIVE

How to Get a Dead Friend Canonized

The Church Loves Saints

How can you get a dead friend canonized?

That can seem like a silly or even disrespectful question but in many ways it's not. In many ways that's exactly what people ask themselves as they take those first tentative steps that lead to the offices of the Congregation for the Causes of Saints.

It could be your friend—your mentor, your teacher, your pastor, your parent—seemed saintly to you, but how do you find out if he or she measures up in the Church's eyes?

That's not easy. And it's not cheap. But the Church is always looking for saints. The Church loves saints. The Church needs saints.

A few years back when the archbishop of Hanoi was in Rome for a meeting, one of his fellow cardinals asked him what the Church could do to help Catholics in war-ravaged Vietnam where religious persecution was common. "Send us *Lives of the Saints*" was the response. (*Go to: "Lives of the Saints: Know Your Audience."*)

Why? Because, he said, more than anything else his people needed to see it's possible to live what Jesus taught and to remain faithful even when it requires heroism.

Saints—much to our amazement and, truth be told, to our

dismay—offer the proof that *anyone* can reach that level of holiness. None of us has a legitimate excuse for not doing what they did.

At the same time, naturally enough, the Church sometimes keeps a sharper eye out for folks who fit a particular profile. To put it crudely, there's a glut on the market in some areas.

Members of the clergy, for example. Lots of saints were bishops or priests. Ditto with founders and foundresses. And nuns. That's not to say these people weren't deserving of canonization, but adding one more to the list doesn't cause much of a stir. (Unless, of course, it's a more contemporary bishop, priest or nun.)

The word is out that, these days, the Holy See is especially interested in the causes of married folks. Proportionately, there aren't many saints who were married. And since so many people are—and since so many couples are choosing to live together outside marriage—it would be good to have some examples of husbands and wives who were saints.

Your To-Do List

Which brings us back to your friend. The one you want to get canonized. Let's call him Bob. And these are the basics:

1. Bob has to be dead. There's no way around this.
2. You can take heart that Bob's cause is going to stand a better chance if he was a husband and dad than if he was an archbishop. This is a new development in saint-making and it's in your favor.

    Let's compare it to publishing. A publisher receives thousands of queries, proposals and manuscripts "over the transom"—that is, unsolicited. All of them end up in what's called the "slush pile."

Unless the editor knows you or you have some other "in," your material sits in the slush pile. Now, it's going to be looked at ... eventually.

But if the company really wants to publish books on dogs and you've sent a manuscript on dogs, then—once an editor sees yours—he's going to pay closer attention to it.

3. So while it's in your favor that Bob was a wonderful husband and father, that's not nearly enough. Unless he was a martyr (and, yes, there are still martyrs for the faith) Bob has to have been more than virtuous. More than a good guy. More even than a really good guy. Bob must have demonstrated "heroic virtue." *(Go to: "What's Heroic Virtue and How Can I Get Me Some?")* Without heroic virtue, he doesn't stand a chance.

4. There has to be grassroots support for your idea. If you're the only one who's saying this, well, that's the end of that. Why? Because—going back to public acclamation in the very early Church—if there is no public acclaiming ... there is no saint.

Then, too, sometimes the people don't want their hero or heroine canonized. (*Go to: "Why Bother?"*)

So what do you do? You get together with other people who knew Bob and agree that he just might have been a saint. Your little group could make a private pilgrimage to his gravesite and have some little memorial cards printed up.(*Go to: "Ten Things You Never Knew About Holy Cards."*) Your little ad hoc committee could also ask people to pray that Bob be canonized and suggest people pray to Bob for help in their own lives.

Now it would be a big boost if Bob had been responsible for some miracles when he was alive but that's not mandatory. Even if he had been, those events would have to be carefully examined and documented further along in the canonization process. But word of his miracles while he was alive—or of his interceding after his death—can attract others to your group, especially those who didn't know about Bob.

(What you're doing is creating a cult—a devotion—that centers on Bob. But this is a *private* devotion. That's very, very important. You can meet and pray in homes or in the cemetery but not in church. That would make what you're doing a *public* devotion.)

5. You want to hang on to Bob's stuff. All of it—everything he owned and used—will be a relic later in the process.

6. You need to get the bishop on board. He's the one who decides, "Say, we ought to look into this whole 'Bob might be a saint' business." Of course, it could be a long time after Bob's death before that happens. The Vatican suggests half a century go by. That way the odds are better that it isn't just you—a single fan—or a couple of people who say this ought to happen.

7. After it gets into the bishop's hands, it's out of yours. Sort of. There's still the matter of finances. You can't buy Bob a canonization, but getting him canonized is going to cost some money. Why? Expenses have to be paid. (*Go to:* "*Check, Please.*") That's another advantage of the grassroots support. Not only can you ask for prayers for Bob's cause but you can ask folks to send a dollar or two to the group.

That's important because while Bob's case moves from the diocese to Rome, someone has to foot the bill. Most likely, that someone is you.

8. Concerned that the bishop will decide against forwarding the case to Rome and poor old Bob will never be declared a Servant of God, much less a blessed or saint? Take heart. You can still celebrate "his" feast day.

In fact you can celebrate a day on the Church's Universal Calendar that's set aside for all your departed loved ones, as well as everyone else in heaven—canonized or not. That's what All Saints' Days is all about. (*Go to: "Calling All Saints ... and Souls."*)

That's St. Bob's Day.

Lives of the Saints: Know Your Audience

Since the Church's earliest times, Christians have recorded and talked about the "lives of the saints." In those first years, the tales of martyrs showed others that a saint was someone who died *for* Christ and *like* Christ.

The lists—the canons—were ways of remembering the names of those men and women "mowed down" by the Roman Empire.

Hagiographies—biographies of saints (with "hagio" coming from the Greek for saint)—remain popular today. Most major Catholic publishing houses—and not a few commercial publishers—sell not only collections but individual books on individual saints. (Perhaps the best-known collection of our own era has been *Butler's Lives of the Saints.*) But what's being written now generally tends to be obviously different from what was penned one hundred or even fifty years ago.

Why?

It's not that the saints have changed. Or that their stories have changed. Rather, what appealed to Catholics a century ago—what inspired them, encouraged them, entertained them—isn't what grabs today's Catholic.

In fact, how the lives of the saints are told is—and always has been—a good reflection on the times in which those lives were written, not just the times during which those lives were led.

An example: St. Martin de Porres (1579–1639), a black Dominican brother who lived in Peru, was known throughout Lima for his piety, his social service and his miracles.

A writer could honestly emphasize any one of those three. Not ignore the others, not downplay them, but not make them the central theme of a book or of an entry in a collection. In fact, Martin's story could focus on:

—Racism and how love can overcome it. (He was the illegitimate son of a Spanish knight and freed Panamanian slave. His father did not always accept Martin or his sister. Nor did members of the local community—or the local church—always treat him respectfully.)

—The need to reach out to the people now referred to as "marginalized." Those on the "edges" of society. (Martin provided for the poor, for the sick, for slaves, for soldiers, for orphans.)

—The central role that personal piety plays in attaining holiness. How there's no substitute for time alone in prayer with God. (He was known for spending nights that way.)

—The miraculous in everyday life. (A "wonder worker," he was famous not only for his cures but for his ability to levitate while in deep prayer and to bilocate—to be in two places at the same time.)

So which was the *real* Martin de Porres? All of them. Which are you more likely to read about these days? Probably, the social worker and community activist who loved so deeply, despite the prejudices he faced.

Flying saints just don't "fly" lately. But they did at one time. During different periods in the Church's history, people *loved* to read about and to hear of saints who performed astounding (or just downright strange) miracles. And of holy men and women whose extreme self-denial we might now consider unhealthy.

Adding to the confusion were "pious legends." As mentioned earlier, these were the stories which people loved to tell and loved to hear, but couldn't be proved.

Or disproved.

Even into the twentieth century, this type of saint's life story was well regarded. These were, after all, very entertaining. Like fables, they had withstood the test of time. And, like fables, generally they had an obvious moral or lesson.

The drawback with this type of biography was that, in an age that values reason, they can seem unreasonable or even childish. It can be too easy to dismiss too many of them the same way the Tooth Fairy is brushed aside.

But ours isn't the first era to say, "Wait a minute." More than three hundred years ago a small group of Jesuits—a half dozen—decided they would examine all the lives of the saints and separate the solid wheat from the fanciful chaff.

Known as the Society of Bollandists, their successors—still only six in number—continue the task of writing the *Acta Sanctorum,* the "Acts of the Saints." (The group is named for its founder, Father John Bolland [1596-1665].) What they showed, and continue to demonstrate, is the Church's saints can withstand that kind of close examination. These men and women don't need hyped-up biographies dripping with the bizarre.

If anything, right from apostolic times, saints were supposed to inspire just the opposite. Look, the stories said, these are "normal" people who love so deeply—both their fellow human beings and their God—they have been able to face torture and death. Live a life of service. Be an instrument of God's miraculous healing. And so on.

One of the twentieth century's most scholarly popes, Pius XI, had been so impressed by the Bollandists and their work when he was still a priest, that later—as pontiff—he used that approach as a model when he set up the historical section in the canonization process. He urged bishops to use those same stringent methods of research when they were looking into causes.

What's Heroic Virtue and How Can I Get Me Some?

Saints still fall into two general categories: martyrs and nonmartyrs. To become a canonized nonmartyr, one has to have demonstrated heroic virtue.

But what does "heroic" mean? And what virtues are we—or rather, is the Vatican—talking about?

"Heroic" means, to use a definition that's not too technical, a lot. A lot of virtue. Enough virtue that it's obvious. Virtue in the morning, virtue in the evening, virtue at supper time. Virtue in public. Virtue in private.

But, again, this doesn't mean perfection. Every saint had his or her faults. And "heroic" doesn't have some Herculean twist to it. A saint doesn't have to be half-human and half-god.

Think about it. What good would that do the rest of us who are 100 percent human?

No, what needs to be shown is a truckload of virtue. But what virtue?

There are seven of them on the saint-makers' list. Faith, hope and love. These are the theological virtues. And prudence, justice, temperance and fortitude. That quartet is known as the cardinal or moral virtues.

Those are the seven "holiness gauges" any investigation wants to check. If the needle is running close to the Big E—for "Empty"—in any of those areas, the investigators are right in assuming something is amiss.

Why? Because these two sets are so interlocked. They make a "complete" person. All of us are expected to possess them. Those being considered for canonization are supposed to have them in Jumbo Size.

You may be more familiar with the first three. Faith, hope and love (or charity)—famous in Scripture and song—are "supernatural." That is, we get them by God's grace. They're a gift. While we can cultivate them (beg God for them and use the amounts he's given us), we can't "create" them. Theologians say they are "infused" in us.

The other four have philosophical roots. While each is written about and demonstrated in the Bible, these "moral virtues" go back to Aristotle, that Greek philosopher of the fourth century before Christ. (Cardinal comes from the Latin for "hinge." St. Ambrose (c. 340–397) is credited with first calling them that. His point was all the other virtues hinge on these four.)

Prudence is another name for wisdom. It doesn't mean being a "prude" in the negative sense that we use the word. It means *not* being a fool.

Justice—or righteousness—is easy to define. It's giving everyone, and seeing to it that everyone gets, a fair shake.

Fortitude is courage. There are no weenie saints. (Despite at-times popular artwork that has made some of them look as if they haven't the strength to snap a twig.) It wasn't just martyrs who displayed courage. All saints, one way or another, did.

And temperance—which here doesn't refer to being a nondrinker—is not going overboard. It's going through life one step at a time. It's not being timid, it's being smart. The nontemperate burn out. It's an attitude that, ideally, the saints used not only in their ministry but in their private lives as well.

As one early Christian writer noted: Extremes meet. If I eat like a pig I feel sick and I can't get anything done. If I eat nothing as a personal penance I feel sick and I can't get anything done. Either way, glutton or misguided ascetic, that is, one who practices self-denial for religious reasons, the result is the same.

"The moral virtues," says the *Catechism of the Catholic Church*, "grow through education, deliberate acts, and perseverance in struggle" [1839].

If we want our prudence, justice, fortitude or temperance to grow stronger, then, to borrow an expression from the sports world, we must "Use it or lose it."

Why Bother?

It might seem that anyone associated with a person who might end up a saint would be hot to start the procedure. But that's not always the case. In some instances the local community doesn't want to "hand over" the process to Rome.

The feeling of "he's already our saint" or "we don't need or want your stamp of approval because we already know what she is" can still be found.

And then there's money. Filthy lucre. This isn't to imply a few Vatican palms have to be greased to get the ball rolling and keep it moving until canonization. Rather, there are legitimate—and not small—expenses that have to be met.

That's why some who have been associated with a likely candidate will say, "Forget about it. She spent her whole life embracing voluntary poverty and would consider this a colossal waste of money." Or, "He never spent a dime on himself and we know he would want any funds to go to those who need it now, not toward this."

Dorothy Day is a good example. The cofounder of the Catholic Worker Movement, she is arguably the most influential American Catholic of the twentieth century. Day died in 1980, but her work continues.

Certainly she wouldn't want money spent on the canon lawyers, historians and such.

That may be true, but ...

The flip side of the argument holds a lot of weight, too. It's not an exaggeration to say that because of her (and fellow founder Peter Maurin), millions of poor people have been fed a hot and hearty meal, have been clothed, have been given a decent place to sleep and have been helped to escape the cycle of poverty.

More than that, they've been given respect—and love.

And those who have food, clothes and a place to stay have been given the opportunity to fulfill Christ's command to find and see him in our less fortunate brothers and sisters. To serve him, in those brothers and sisters.

And to learn countless lessons from those whom they came to help. (Was there ever a sincere volunteer who didn't say, "I get a lot more out of it than I put into it"?)

Would the Catholic Worker Movement have prospered without Day's personality? Without her convictions? Without her strength? Without her?

Well, of course, any authentic Christian charity is inspired by Christ and guided by the Holy Spirit. But ...

Day did her part, too.

And—the argument for canonization goes—that help (her "intervention") can continue now. And others, learning of "St. Dorothy" and the work she and her followers did (and do), can be moved to do the same. Just as so much was accomplished because there was a Dorothy Day, more can—and should—be done because there is a "St. Dorothy Day."

And ... a *big* "and" here ... and Catholics and others of the twenty-first century *need* a saint who was a layperson. Who floundered in her younger years. (While in her early adulthood, Day got pregnant outside of marriage and had an abortion.) Who consciously chose to become a Catholic, consciously "chose God"—or probably, more accurately, realized God had "chosen" her just as he chooses each of us.

But even after her radical conversion, she was never a goody-two-shoes. Day was a blunt, forceful, faith-filled woman.

She doesn't need to be canonized, the counterargument goes. *We* need her to be canonized. We need to hear her story again and again and again. We need to realize she can be prayed to. We need to have "St. Dorothy Day" parishes where school children learn of her. We need to have "St. Dorothy's" feast day to help us stop and take stock of where we are and what we do when it comes to serving the most needy among us.

We need her now just as Catholic Workers and hangers-on needed her when she was living. And her message—which is, of course, the same as the message of St. Francis of Assisi, the same as the message Jesus brought—needs to be broadcast as widely as possible.

That's what canonization can do. Especially in our own time, with the sensibilities that we value, Day would not be put on a pedestal and become unapproachable. She would be in soup kitchens, in houses of hospitality, on picket lines, in Catholic homes.

She would be where she belongs.

She would be with us.

Ten Things You Never Knew About Holy Cards

1. Holy cards—as we know them today—trace their history back to the work of a German map inspector named Aloys Senefelder (1771–1834). He created the printing process known as lithography. Senefelder had been fiddling around while trying to come up with a way for printing his own dramatic writings. In 1796, he discovered a method of marking a stone with wax which he called "chemical printing."

   Versatile and cheap, it rapidly gained popularity in Europe, and within twenty-five years European printers were producing countless lithographed devotional prints. Industrialization upped the quality of prints available to worldwide markets.

2. In the 1800s French companies cranked out a huge amount of Catholic religious material, and by 1862 at least 120 firms marketed mass-produced religious goods, including novenas (special prayers usually said over nine days) and holy cards.

3. These cards used a style that came to be known as *l'art Saint-Sulpice*. It made all saints—even a robust fisherman like Peter—look soft and bunny-eyed. Art critics howled. Catholics lapped them up.

4. By then the most popular use of holy cards among American Catholics was as funeral mementos.

5. From the 1930s through the 1960s, the popularity of devotions to Mary and the saints boosted production and distribution.

6. In the 1940s—really—women began to eat holy cards of Mary. Seriously. They would peck away at the edges first and then swallow the center. An Irish company made a variety of cards, each compressed into a pellet that slid right down.

7. In those days before Vatican II, a holy card was a standard gift or reward in Catholic schools and religious education classes.

8. Right after the council, the market dropped off. Saints' images were replaced by Scripture quotes and Christian symbols. Now sales are edging up again.

9. There's also a market now for old cards. Some folks collect them. Especially prized are "relic cards," often distributed as a way of promoting a cause. These would feature a snippet of cloth touched to the relics of the Servant of God or a tiny piece of the person's clothing or other effects.

10. In some ways the equivalent of a "rookie card," relic cards of some now-canonized folks that carry the designation "Servant of God," "Venerable" or "Blessed" are hot stuff among collectors.

Check, Please

In his excellent book *Making Saints*, Kenneth L. Woodward took a look at some budgets.

Woodward reported that for the cause for St. Elizabeth Ann Seton (America's first native-born saint) from the time it was introduced in 1929 until her canonization in 1975, the bill was about $250,000.

But there's no price list.

Some causes would involve a lot of travel and call for the scrutinizing of a lot of the Servant of God's writing. Others wouldn't.

Then, too, those costs are spread over decades, if not centuries.

And a lot of the work is done by volunteers or given to priests and sisters whose expenses are covered but whose wages are meager.

Needless to say, if a member of a religious order is working for the founder's or foundress' cause, expenses are minimal.

So what would be some expenses? Witnesses who have to travel. Physicians who have to examine records of purported miracles. "Relators'" salaries. (Being a relator is not the road to riches.) Historians and theologians. (Neither of them are on the gravy train either.) Phone bills. Publishing a hundred or so copies of a positio (the cause's paperwork) that can run more than one thousand pages. (Much more costly back in pre-photocopy days.) The ceremonies themselves. Beatification and canonization. Travel and hotel expenses for those attending them. The costs for printing programs.

And a gift for the Holy Father. A gesture. How much is a gesture? Woodward reported that when Mother Katharine

Drexel was beatified, her order donated $10,000 "to the Holy Father for the poor."

It's safe to say that's how he used it. Unlike in past centuries when royalty and rich folk did try to grease the skids in many ways. Woodward says records show the consultors for one nineteenth-century cause were given spices, sugar, chocolate and other treats that were in short supply in Rome because of a continental blockade.

So who foots the bill now? A diocese or religious order may pay for most of it. But, one way or another, a lot of the funding comes from the people who support the cause. Their contributions to the promoters of the cause make it possible.

Of course some causes have an easier time raising money. Some may have a surplus. When that happens, excess is used to support the type of ministry the Servant of God was into during his or her life. And it goes to help out other causes that aren't as flush. Those originating in Third World countries, for instance.

Calling All Saints ... and Souls

The Church says November 1 is the feast for everyone who is in heaven. (After all, everyone there is a saint. Some are canonized, some aren't.)

What this means is, not only is it a celebration for all those big-name saints and all the ones on the local calendar, it's the day for all your own loved ones, too.

It's the feast day for your friends and family members who have died.

But how do you really know if they're in heaven? Well,

we assume that. But, just in case, November 2 is the feast of All Souls. It's for all the departed who are still in purgatory. (We talked about that in chapter one.)

In years past, a strict procedure was followed for praying for loved ones on that day. Particular prayers were said in a church, with only one soul served at a time.

The faithful would privately say those prayers and then walk out of and back into the building to begin identical prayers for another dear soul.

If in the past, there was too much emphasis on purgatory—with the horrible image of dearly departed suffering for years, decades or centuries—there may be too little mention of it now.

Now we like to assume our loved ones zip straight through the Pearly Gates.

Either extreme may be inaccurate. God only knows.

And, fortunately for us, his justice is tempered by his mercy.

He loves us with an infinite love.

Ask St. Joe:
Who Canonized You?

Dear St. Joe:

How is it you're a saint but, tradition says, you died before Jesus did?

Stickler for Details

Dear Stickler:

I'm not the only one. John the Baptist is another and so are Jesus' maternal grandparents Joachim and Anne.

We're considered saints because we, like others, were given special devotion in the early days of the Church.

St. Joe

Quote / Unquote

"I do believe every soul has a tendency toward God."
—Dorothy Day (1897–1980)

CHAPTER SIX

Miracles, Visions and the Archangel Melvin

Prove It

The problem with miracles is that we really like them and we really don't like them. We want to believe in this form of divine intervention and we want to stay true to that generally accepted scientific outlook that says "there's a logical explanation for everything."

Odds are we don't even realize we are a product of our own times. But then most members of every age and culture are.

The Church is big on miracles. It always has been. The Old and New Testaments are filled with them, even if they didn't use that particular word to describe what was happening. (*Go to: "Miracles in the Bible."*)

These days in the saint-making process, a Servant of God, having been found to be heroically virtuous and declared "venerable," is going to remain at that level unless and until some miracles are attributed to him or her.

In a sense, it's giving God the final say. "We think she's a saint but we aren't going to declare it so without your stamp of approval." The Church forwards the cause to God's in-box and if it stays there forever, so be it.

As mentioned in chapter five, under the old system of canonization it took two miracles to be declared blessed and two more for sainthood. (Or for martyrs, given a bye for beatification, only two for canonization.) Now it's one and one.

It may seem the Church has made the process easier. But that's not really so. If anything, it can be harder to have even one miracle attributed to a Servant of God because advances in science make it more difficult to prove a miracle occurred.

And while, without a doubt, it's God who performs the miracle, it's people—the cult, the devotees of a particular Servant of God or blessed—who prime the pump. So to speak. They ask for that person's intervention. For that person's particular help. And as promoters of the cause, they strongly encourage others to do the same.

But any "miracle" has to be clearly attributable to that particular person. If you said prayers to a variety of saints and to a Servant of God and then something happened, there would be no way of "proving" it was the Servant of God who intervened.

If, however, you stormed heaven by praying to Jesus and the servant, then the servant is eligible for the credit. Why? Because, ultimately, all miracles depend on God.

But in this day and age, do people *really* pray to a particular Servant of God or blessed? Oh, yes. The miracle attributed to Edith Stein—canonized in 1998—is a good example. (*Go to: "Edith Stein and Young Teresia Benedicta."*)

Once that intervention has been received, or it's believed to have been received, the Vatican's medical consultants (since almost all miracles these days are cures) look into it and decide if there's no scientific explanation for what has happened.

How do they do that? Very carefully.

The sixty-plus physicians of the Consulta Medica are top-of-the-line doctors who live in Rome. Panels of five examine particular cases, working in a way that's similar to a medical review board. They look at the charts, the X rays, the reports. They talk to witnesses and health-care professionals.

And they vote.

Not looking for a miracle, they render a judgment on whether or not a cure had—or could have had—a medical or natural cause. If a majority agrees, that's the conclusion they report.

But it isn't just "modern" cases they examine. Some may be centuries old. And some, coming from remote or medically primitive locations, may have little in the way of documentation. Still, working with what they have—and not cutting corners—they render the soundest decision possible.

Back in the Day

It used to be easier, of course. People by and large used to believe in miracles. Long before the "laws" of science or nature became known, it was assumed God stepped in and did marvelous things. And those closest to him, the holy men and women who would become saints, were his instruments both before and after their deaths.

Throughout the first millennium and beyond, folks *loved* stories of miracles. The more the merrier. The more ... outlandish, the merrier. With little understanding of science and a facility at spreading tall tales (at a speed, it could be argued, that rivaled today's e-mail) people had a way of making stories grow.

This isn't to say some accounts weren't true. And others based in truth. But....

But it was only in the last four centuries—when the Holy See really started to get a handle on controlling the canonization process—that *proving* miracles and relying on them for proof of sainthood were made part of that process.

Even today miracles tend to have a bad reputation. For example, there are the reports of Jesus appearing in a door screen or of Mary being spotted on the back of a highway road sign. In the public's mind, those "sightings" are lumped together with claims made by saints. Not a few saints said they saw or heard Christ or his Mother. Not a few are reputed to have appeared to others after the saint's death.

And while Scripture also reports apparitions, perhaps the most familiar and accepted response for us belongs to the apostle Thomas: I'll believe it when *I* see it. (Of course, there is Jesus' reply: "Blessed are those who have not seen but still believe.")

St. Stephen, the deacon killed by a mob, had an apparition. That's what Luke reports in his Acts of the Apostles. As the good and holy man met death, he saw heaven open up and "the Son of Man standing at the right hand of God."

Then there was Saul. The vigorous persecutor of Christians who was knocked to the ground on his way to Damascus. (Artists have portrayed him tumbling from a horse but Luke doesn't mention that.) He saw a bright flash and heard Jesus speak to him. And then he was blind for a while.

Check It Out

Saul, soon to be Paul, needed to talk to someone about what he had seen and heard. In a sense, that's been the approach the Church has continued to use when it comes to apparitions.

You may have had one—it's a possibility, after all—but it's best to bounce that idea off someone wiser.

That's certainly not to say other people always believe folks who claim visions. More often than not, the reaction among the visionaries' peers are:

1. Why would God (or Mary or a saint) choose you?
2. You're only doing this to get attention.
3. You're nuts.

In the cases of those who later go on to become blesseds or saints, the laughers and nay-sayers are proven wrong. Those, of course, are the stories we read about in the lives of the saints. (The Sacred Heart visiting St. Margaret Mary Alacoque, for example.)

Check out the movie *The Song of Bernadette* sometime. Actor Vincent Price is superb as the town official trying to cow the poor simple French girl into contradicting her own testimony.

But what the film isn't so good at is showing how once word of her case became known in the area, all sorts of young girls were "seeing things." (And a century later, after the movie was in theaters, more than a few youngsters reported sightings.)

What we tend to forget is that just about every age produces folks who claim to see visions. (And, I think, some of them really do.)

In my own work as a journalist, I interviewed a woman who truly believed the "Archangel Melvin" spoke to her through automatic handwriting. (She would hold pen to paper and this spirit would guide her hand.) She had put together a collection of her—or his—words into a fat, self-published book. Others in her immediate circle believed what it said.

Was it Truth with a capital T? It wasn't for me to judge, but I had my doubts. I believe she was sincere but I had no faith in Melvin. Fortunately, as we mentioned before, the Church is very specific when it comes to "private revelations."

It doesn't demand anyone believe them. You aren't required to say, yes, Mary appeared to Juan Diego in the sixteenth century or to Bernadette Soubirous in the nineteenth or to three Portuguese children at the start of the twentieth.

It certainly isn't mandatory to believe in Melvin.

What the Church Says

To quote the *Catechism:*

"Throughout the ages, there have been so-called 'private' revelations, some of which have been recognized by the authority of the Church. They do not belong, however, to the deposit of faith. It is not their role to improve or complete Christ's definitive Revelation, but to help live more fully by it in a certain period of history. Guided by the Magisterium of the Church, the *sensus fidelium* knows how to discern and welcome in these revelations whatever constitutes an authentic call of Christ or his saints to the Church.

"Christian faith cannot accept 'revelations' that claim to surpass or correct the Revelation of which Christ is the fulfillment ..." [67].

That final point is key: A private revelation—if authentic—isn't going to contradict what Jesus taught. It isn't going to one-up Christ.

It takes time and wisdom and grace to sort out the visionaries from the wannabes and the con artists. That's why the Church is cautious when there's news of someone seeing something somewhere.

It may be miraculous. And it may be malarkey.

And the Church doesn't rush to decide.

But keep in mind a person isn't declared a saint because he or she claimed to have seen Mary or Jesus or angels or saints. Not even if the Church says that claim appears to be legitimate. (*Go to: "Proving You Had a Vision."*) Obviously, some folks who had visions have been declared saints. But not because of those visions. (And maybe having a vision or some other inexplicable event [*Go to: "Extraordinary Gifts."*] isn't as unusual as we tend to think it is. It could very well be some folks—maybe even you—truly have them but don't talk about them.)

When it comes to visions and saints, this is what's important to keep in mind: A vision is not on the checklist for canonization. Heroic virtue is.

Miracles in the Bible

The Hebrews of the Old Testament had no word for "miracle." In their language it was a sign, a wonder, a portent (prophecy) or something that went beyond what was ordinary or expected.

But just what did they expect? What did they consider "ordinary," the way we would view the laws of nature?

They believed God caused all the events that we would call "natural." A thunderstorm, an earthquake, a drought. Most non-Hebrews assumed such things were the gods fighting with each other. The Israelites, believing in one God, figured these disasters or near-disasters were the result of human beings not being in sync with the will of Yahweh.

Both Hebrews and pagans were also big-time believers in magic. Not sleight of hand but what they assumed was the real McCoy. But, the Israelites said, God was more powerful, which was why his prophets could outdo any magicians.

In the New Testament, what we would call "miracles" are called "powers" or works of power. The authors also use a Greek word that means sign. Miracles are signs of God's intervention. They are signs that Jesus is the Son of God, the Savior.

But "power" is the more common word. That's important because the point was Jesus has the power not only to save someone from the evil of sin but to cure the body. This power resides in him but he gives it to his apostles (who can also perform signs and wonders) and, after he ascends into heaven, it's given to the Church, too, in which Jesus continues to live.

So this power, Scripture scholars say, is a part of the lasting presence of Jesus in the Church and a "sign" of God working through it. They add that this isn't to say every "miracle" described in the New Testament could stand up to literary or historical scrutiny. But there were signs which still can't be explained. Not even with contemporary rationalizing.

There is a trend these days to offer "logical," warm, fuzzy explanations for New Testament miracles. The few loaves of bread and couple of fish didn't *really* feed thousands of people. (When others saw that Jesus was being so generous, they started to share their own little stashes, too.) Or folks weren't actually *physically* healed, they just felt so much better psychologically.

Again, we don't like miracles because we can't explain them. Not without that darn God-angle. And a lot of us are just a little too sophisticated for that, aren't we?

But, the evangelists write, those few loaves and couple of fish fed everyone. With leftovers. There's no mention, no hint, of anyone else chipping in.

And do we really think if Jesus offered only psychological healing, folks would have come by the thousands to see him, to hear him, to touch him and have him touch them? ("Let's take poor cousin Benjamin to see Jesus. Old Ben will still be lame but he'll *feel* so much better about himself.")

Not very likely.

No, those healing miracles are one of two categories for the wonders worked by Jesus. The other is nature miracles. He has say over the wind, the rain, the sea.

He has the ability not only to forgive sins but to take away the consequences of sin and evil. To take away human suffering (brought on by what we would call nature or as a result of sin).

But the nature miracles aren't some sort of magic act. They show Jesus has the power and the will to save.

Bottom line: A miracle then, or now, is never simply a rabbit out of a hat. A miracle then, or now, teaches us something about God. About what God is like. About his plan for salvation.

Edith Stein and Young Teresia Benedicta

Edith Stein was born into a Jewish family in Germany in 1891. She abandoned her religion in 1904 and became a self-proclaimed atheist. A brilliant student, she excelled in her studies and, after earning a doctorate in 1916, emerged as one of Europe's brightest philosophers.

After studying the works of St. Thomas Aquinas, and being captivated by the writings of St. Teresa of Avila, she entered the Catholic Church in 1922 and joined the Carmelite Order twelve years later.

As the Nazis gained power in her homeland, Sister Teresa Benedicta—her professed name—was smuggled into the

Netherlands in 1938. Later that country came under the Third Reich and in 1942 she and her sister Rosa (who had also converted) were arrested with fellow "non-Aryan Catholics."

That sweep was retaliation for the Dutch bishops opposing Hitler.

She was taken to Auschwitz where she died in the gas chamber on August 9, 1942.

After the war her writings were collected and published. Her cause was opened in 1962 and Pope John Paul II beatified her in 1987 during a visit to Germany.

While she clearly had a following, Blessed Edith had no gravesite. There was no tomb to visit. Her body had been incinerated like millions of others. That, some people noted, would make it more difficult to promote her cause and encourage others to seek a miracle through her intercession.

Enter Emmanuel Charles McCarthy, an American priest of the Melkite Church (a Byzantine rite in communion with Rome). Like other Eastern-rite Catholic Churches, the Melkites ordain married men. Even married men with children. In McCarthy's case, ten of them.

So Emmanuel Charles McCarthy was ordained on August 9, 1981. But it wasn't until three years later that it came to his attention that happened to be Blessed Edith's feast day.

Inspired by her story and deeply impressed by her words, McCarthy and his wife decided to name their new baby girl Teresia Benedicta. ("Teresia" being the form Blessed Edith herself used.)

In 1987, two-year-old Teresia Benedicta happened onto a box of over-the-counter pain medication samples and ate a lethal dose. As the toddler lay dying of liver failure in the hospital, McCarthy contacted a series of people—folks to whom he had given retreats over the years—and asked them to start phone trees with others to get as many people as possible to pray to Blessed Edith for his daughter's recovery.

Two days after Teresia Benedicta entered the hospital, McCarthy was scheduled to begin directing a three-day retreat in another state. On the night before he was supposed to begin—unable to sleep despite having had no rest for forty-eight hours—he happened to notice a book on the floor near his bed. He picked it up to put it back on a shelf and as he glanced down a line jumped out at him.

The book was about St. Teresa of Avila, the reformer of Blessed Edith's order. The passage said that Jesus told St. Teresa, at a trying time in her life: "You take care of my business and I'll take care of your business."

McCarthy took it as a sign to get on with the retreat. Once there, he told no one that, hour by hour, his daughter's condition was worsening. The retreat concluded at 1:00 P.M. Central Time on March 24, 1987, making it 2:00 P.M. back at the hospital in Boston. At that point he told the retreatants about his daughter. They gasped, cried and prayed. McCarthy returned home to find that his daughter had made a miraculous recovery.

It was ten months later, at the request of the Carmelite Order, that McCarthy obtained Teresia Benedicta's hospital records. On March 24, 1987, at 2:00 P.M., the doctor had written on the toddler's chart: "This child has made a remarkable recovery."

The Consulta Medica determined there was no medical explanation.

The Vatican Congregation for the Causes of Saints decided it was a miracle.

Pope John Paul II canonized Edith Stein on October 11, 1998.

McCarthy has termed the miracle of his daughter's recovery "the infinitely delicate hand of God."

That's not a bad definition.

"Either," he wrote, "everything is mindless, purposeless, meaningless, unguided chance or all is grace: purposeful, meaningful, divinely guided activity meant to communicate God's love, God's truth and God's plan for the salvation of humanity."

Proving You Had a Vision

The Church says there are three possible causes of extraordinary or paranormal phenomena.

1. God. (This would be good.)
2. The devil. (This would be bad. *Go to: Is Satan Real?"*)
3. Nature. (This would be kind of boring.)

And, unless proven otherwise, it presumes the cause is No. 2 or No. 3.

So if you had a vision, how would you prove it was of a divine origin? You wouldn't. The Church would.

First, the bishop in your diocese—the location where your apparitions are being reported—would be the one responsible to begin any investigation. Because the phenomenon would have to be looked at from a number of different angles (theological, psychological, pathological and medical), he would set up a commission of experts from those areas.

The commission would want to know about you. All

about you. Your physical, emotional and moral qualities would be investigated to see if there was anything that would raise questions about your credibility. (Say, for instance, you had a brain tumor. Or you had a tendency to overdramatize common situations. Or your major source of income was selling souvenirs to pilgrims flocking to the spot where you claimed to see whatever it was you saw.)

The commission would also check to see if your claims were consistent. Or if, over time, the "facts" changed.

It would also look to see if these apparitions had produced any "spiritual fruits" in you or in others. Have they made you or others better people?

And the commission would reach one of three conclusions:

1. The alleged apparition seems to be of divine origin.

2. The alleged apparition is definitely not of divine origin so it is presumed to have a diabolical or natural cause.

3. The commission can't decide because there isn't enough evidence and so the case needs to remain open as long as there is that uncertainty.

If the diocesan commission concludes there seems to be a divine origin for what you've been claiming to see, then the findings are bumped up to the Holy See for a final decision. But even if the Church gives it official recognition, it remains a "private" revelation.

Extraordinary Gifts

The "extraordinary gifts" of saints have been divided up into a number of different categories. "Extraordinary gifts" is the term that's used to designate unusual and mysterious phenomena that go beyond natural human powers.

It was Pope Benedict XIV in his *"De Servorum Dei beatificatione et Beatorum canonizatione"* (see chapter four) that came up with the basic rules for determining if a gift had a supernatural, natural or diabolic cause.

But what are those gifts?

—*Visions.*

—*Locutions.* Simply put, words. A message. It could be the audio track to that video vision.

—*Revelations.* A truth for the good of the Church or for individuals.

—*Reading of hearts.* "Infused" knowledge of the secret thoughts or internal state of other people without previous communication.

—*Hierognosis.* The ability to immediately recognize a person, place or thing is holy or blessed and to distinguish it from those that are not.

—*Stigmata.* The spontaneous appearance of the wounds of the crucified Christ.

—*Tears of blood and bloody sweat.* Reminiscent of Jesus in the Garden of Gethsemane.

—*Flames of love.* Burning sensations in the body, usually by the heart. (It may be so intense cold applications are used or clothing is scorched.)

—*Exchange of hearts.* This, in a vision, is the extraction of a mystic's heart and the substitution of another's, presumably Christ's.

—*Levitation.* The body suspended in the air, contrary to

gravity. It usually occurs during "ecstasy"—that is, when the mystic is in deep personal prayer.

—*Agility.* The apparent instantaneous movement of a body from one place to another without going through the space between those two spots.

—*Telekinesis.* The movement of an inanimate object through space without the help of anyone or anything natural.

—*Bilocation.* Being simultaneously present in two different places at the same time.

—*Compenetration of bodies.* A body passing through another material object.

—*Inedia.* Total abstinence from nourishment that goes beyond what a body could endure.

—*Mystical aureoles.* Light coming from the head, face or body (especially during prayer). Real halos!

—*Incorruptibility.* A corpse that doesn't decompose or even remains soft and flexible and gives off a pleasant fragrance.

Is Satan Real?

Is Satan real? You bet. Among the things the *Catechism* says about the devil are:

—"The Church teaches that Satan was at first a good angel, made by God ..." [391][a] ... who, given the gift of free choice, "radically and irrevocably *rejected* God and his reign" [392].

—"The power of Satan is ... not infinite. He is only a creature, powerful from the fact that he is pure [that is, 100 percent] spirit, but still a creature. He cannot prevent the building up of God's reign. Although Satan may act in the world out of hatred for God and his kingdom in Christ Jesus, and although his action may cause grave injuries—of a spiritual nature and, indirectly, even of a physical nature—to each man and to society, the action is permitted by divine providence which with strength and gentleness guides human and cosmic history. It is a great mystery that providence should permit diabolical activity, but 'we know that in everything God works for good with those who love him'" [395].[10]

Ask St. Joe:
What Did You See?

Dear St. Joe:
   Did you have visions?

                        Interested in Miracles and Such

Dear Interested:
   You can assume that when I prayed "Lord, tell me what to do," God answered, "In your dreams!"

                                            St. Joe

Quote / Unquote

"The faith of Christ believed by the saints and handed down to us has been marked by the seal of God shown in works no creature can perform. These are the miracles by which Christ has confirmed holy apostolic doctrine."

                        —St. Thomas Aquinas (1225–74)

CHAPTER SEVEN

Relics: I Left My Heart in ...

How Much for a Dead Movie Star's Dress?

In many ways the idea of relics offends our twenty-first-century sensibilities. In others, it makes perfect sense.

Hard-core sports aficionados treasure dirt from a World Series batter's box. Elvis impersonators bid frantically when an item "The King" owned comes up for sale at auction. Bibliophiles—book lovers—fondly caress a text written and autographed by a long-dead poet or novelist. Archaeologists and historians consider an ancient pot shard or broken tea cup a treasure.

More than that, music fans surround—and sometimes nearly crush—the latest singing sensation, grasping for any memento: a bit of cloth, a button, a lock—*ouch!*—of hair.

We might not really *understand* a person or group's fascination with items once owned by someone famous or long dead, but we're familiar with it. It doesn't surprise us.

But relics go beyond that. Relics seem to have a certain ghoulish aspect to them at first glance. Left unexplained, they don't quite make sense to us.

I remember hearing that a lot at a museum exhibit that included both relics and reliquaries. (*Go to: "A Box for Bones."*) The items were on loan from the Basilica of St. Francis in Assisi, Italy. The showing was part of a U.S. tour to raise money for the earthquake-damaged building.

In this silver box, explained a small sign next to one case, was the finger of St. Andrew. Or, rather, it had been. The finger was no longer there but, from the museum's perspective, the point was the artistry of the box, not the digit of the apostle.

There were other reliquaries, too. Most empty, some still containing a sliver of this saint or that. One was even said to contain a thorn from Jesus' crown.

So what's the deal with relics? That's a very good question. It's one that, down through the centuries, some of the Church's foremost theologians and saints have asked ... and answered.

One, Two, Three

But before we get into the history of relics, maybe we should explain exactly what it is we're talking about. The word "relic" comes from the Latin for "remains."

These days, relics fall into three categories:

—First class: This is a part of a saint's body.

—Second class: This is an item worn or used by a saint during his or her lifetime. It could be a pair of sandals, a rosary, a pencil and so on.

—Third class: This is an item that has been touched to a first-class relic. Usually, a bit of cloth.

Scripture scholars say there's no "cult of relics"—that is, devotion shown to relics—in the Old Testament. And those items didn't receive much attention in the New. But while the apostles themselves maintained that Jewish approach and attitude toward relics, new converts in St. Paul's time fought over handkerchiefs he had touched. Why? Because when the pieces of cloth "were brought to the sick, their diseases left them, and the evil spirits came out of them."

Historians say there's clear-cut evidence that in the middle of the second century people were venerating the relics of St. Polycarp, a bishop of Smyrna (now in modern-day Turkey). Then, too, the Romans were very respectful of the dead. So much so they usually allowed condemned criminals to be buried. There was an exception. If the person had committed a crime against the state or its ruler, the magistrates could forbid that the body be given to friends or family, or given to anyone, for that matter.

Since all Christians were considered traitors for their failure to worship the emperor or the state's gods, no one could legally claim martyrs' bodies. That was why, often, the remains were stolen or snatched away for burial by fellow Christians.

But the writing about St. Polycarp shows something new. Veneration was no longer private and implicit. Now there was a public and explicit cult. The folks in Smyrna let everyone know they had a particular devotion to the remains of their beloved bishop. And once they had that, they needed to justify what they were doing.

The community stressed the "subordinate character" of the veneration of martyrs. These holy men and women weren't on a par with Christ, and the respect shown to their relics didn't match—couldn't match, shouldn't match—that shown to God. Rather, Polycarp was honored because this holy person had been "a disciple and imitator of Christ." So each year on the anniversary of his death, the people went to his grave and paid their respects.

There was no shortage of martyrs—or of relics—during those early centuries. That form of veneration became common and, historians say, it doesn't appear to have been opposed by the bishops. Still, it wasn't until the third century that a liturgy—specific prayers at the Eucharist—was a part of the ceremony. Relics were just collected and reverently buried.

In the middle of the third century, St. Cyprian of Carthage—a bishop—said venerating the instruments used to torture and kill the martyrs was all right because their bodies had made those items holy. In the fourth century, St. Basil—a Doctor of the Church—wrote in detail about the official ceremonies held on an anniversary.

Not everyone agreed. Some theologians didn't want any "external" cult. Others considered it pagan to show such respect to an object.

Meanwhile, Back at Headquarters

In Rome, relics had become associated with liturgical worship. Venerating the dead was the only form of public worship that could be freely practiced during those times of persecution. It only made sense, then, that Christians gathered near tombs to honor the dead and, naturally enough, sometimes that gathering included a liturgical celebration. (*Go to: "The Not-So-Secret Catacombs."*)

Once Christianity was no longer illegal, that practice became more common until—as mentioned before—churches were built over the graves of martyrs, including the Basilicas of St. Peter and St. Paul in Rome.

Over the next couple hundred years, venerating martyrs' relics grew as a liturgical cult and theologians looked at what was happening and said it made sense. Tombs were opened and items were touched to the body or bones. Then these relics—called "brandea"—were distributed throughout the community.

(They were what today are known as third-class relics.) People kept *brandea* in little cases and hung them around their necks.

Still, there were opposing points of view by the big-name theologians of that period. Those against honoring relics continued to say it was nothing less than idolatry, even though, by then, writers had pointed out the difference between worship (latria) and veneration (dulia), which we talked about in chapter two.

Those who said it was all right argued:

1. Christians see the saints in the relics they venerate. Since these martyrs were saints, their bodies were sanctified—that is, made holy.

2. The holiness of the martyrs makes their relics precious and those relics remind folks the saints should be models.

3. God works miracles through the martyrs' relics. Because his power is shown in those items, they can be venerated.

4. Relics are the remains of friends who, now saints, are close to God.

In the seventh century St. Isidore of Seville (later declared a Doctor of the Church) compiled the Church's teaching on relics, but what new Christians—those in the north who had recently converted—*really* cared about was the miracles those items were said to be producing. Especially the wonders reportedly happening on a martyr's feast day.

And already, Church councils were pointing out to bishops that abuses were taking place with regard to relics. (Relics were, and would remain, a great way for the unscrupulous to make a fast buck.)

At this point, historians say, it's important to realize that what was happening in the East didn't match what was going on in the West.

In the East, bodies were dug up, cut up and moved from place to place. These translations were a Very Big Deal. Emperors wanted to have their time in office marked by such an event. Constantinople, Alexandria and Antioch—each a major city—boasted relics relocated from the boonies.

By the fifth century, dismembering a body and dividing up the bones was considered perfectly acceptable. Why? Because, in the East, Christians believed the soul was totally present everywhere in the body and so every part was of equal worth.

At the same time, in the West, there were laws against messing around with graves. The popes agreed with that and so translations were the exception rather than the rule. One needed a very good reason to move a body.

Or one had to be very sneaky.

That was the case until the eighth century when the city of Rome lightened up and the popes followed suit. In no time at all, a lot of translations were given a papal OK. In Italy, the result was that a lot of bodies were dismembered and relics dispersed. Outside Italy, where there weren't many martyrs, brandea were popping up all over the place until nonmartyr saints—and an increase in first-class relics—became more common.

Pilgrims' Progress

The veneration of relics didn't just affect Church life. The custom of pilgrimages—of going to visit a gravesite or body—began to have all sorts of economic, cultural and social ramifications.

A church or monastery that featured the remains of a popular saint—which might mean one to whom miracles were being attributed—became a Mecca (to borrow a metaphor from our

Muslim brothers and sisters) for visitors. And, as any tourist town knows, travelers come with money burning holes in their pockets. They need a place to stay, meals to eat and souvenirs to bring back home.

It was also during the Middle Ages (the Middle Ages were, roughly, A.D. 500 to 1500) that more relics became available because:

1. Big pieces were divided into smaller pieces.
2. New relics were being discovered.
3. Crooks were making "relics."

Think about it. Your little town wants a relic and here's this fellow—who seems so sincere and has all the necessary paper-work—with the leg bone of a second century martyr. Now you may be very naïve and really believe he's telling the truth. Or you may be more skeptical but realize if you don't buy it, folks in the next town will and pilgrims will be spending their money there instead of here.

Either way, you're inclined to make the purchase.

In the eleventh century, the Church started to make laws about translations to protect relics. One reason was that con-querors from the North and East were swooping in and taking whatever they wanted, whenever they wanted. The other reason was that relics had become a business.

By the eighth and ninth centuries, the city of Rome—which had fallen on hard times—had let its cemeteries go to pot. Pilgrims assumed every bone in every catacomb was a saint's, and popes were giving away whole bodies to hotshot visitors. Religious orders seemed convinced their success depended on whose relics they had, and they wanted some to razzle-dazzle the natives in missionary territory who might be tempted to revert to their old idols.

Popes tried to control all that was happening but they couldn't. Finally Paschal I (817–824) said the catacombs would be completely cleaned out and all relics would be placed in churches in Rome. While that was an admirable idea, its execution was sloppy. Even now, many of those bones have never been identified.

The dawn of the second millennium brought another wrinkle: the Crusades. These were the Christian armies bent on reclaiming the Holy Land from the Muslims. While their intentions may have been noble—or considered noble at the time—these soldiers had a tendency to siege and sack any "foreign" city along the way, including ones which were "Christian." Relics were taken from Constantinople, Antioch and Jerusalem and sent back to Western churches and cathedrals.

Historians do say that, to the Crusaders' credit, the looters were more interested in the relics than in the costly reliquaries that had held them.

Time for New Rules

This flood of "new" relics made it easier for con men to peddle their wares. To stem the flow, horror stories about what happened to such fellows were spread around. (Shades of Indiana Jones and the lost ark!) Finally, in 1274, the Council of Lyons said no new relics could be venerated without the pope's approval.

The official practice became:

Once a relic was discovered and deemed genuine, it was put into a church or chapel as close as possible to the altar. In fact, the martyrs' tombs were considered altars. Dead saints were no longer buried but left out to be seen and touched in tombs that were really very fancy reliquaries. These were placed above or behind the altar.

Then, before long, the rule was that for an altar to be dedicated, it had to contain the relics of martyrs. For new churches, the pastor had to ask the bishop or pope for relics of the saint in whose name the building was being dedicated. There's still a similar requirement. (*Go to: "Altar Stones" and "St. Peter and St. Paul Come to North Carolina."*)

One big reason relics were so popular in the late Middle Ages was that folks considered them very powerful. Shrines—tomb sites, really, or churches built over graves—were top sites for pilgrims. Even at a time when travel was difficult, expensive and dangerous, people flocked to shrines, especially on the feast days of the saints laid out there.

Feast days became religious holidays. And that didn't just mean no work, but processions featuring relics being carried through the town. It meant fairs and other gatherings that—historians say—played a key role in the exchange of ideas, information, styles and customs.

Then, too, a lot of government events—swearing in new officials, for example, or signing a treaty—included a tip-o'-the-hat to the local church's or monastery's relics. And those "local saints" were regularly called upon to protect citizens from disease. It wasn't uncommon for people to touch relics to the particular part of the body that was sick.

Again, abuses sprang up. But theologians knew they didn't have the power to stop that from happening and instead focused their attention on developing doctrine concerning relics. At the same time, cathedrals were being built and Masses written in honor of the saints. But never in honor of a saint's relics.

By now it had been many, many centuries since the Fathers of the Church (those early theologians) had tackled the—not problem but concern—that relics could cause and so the "scholastics" took a crack at explaining them. (The scholastics were the theologians of the late Middle Ages.) Most reiterated what the early writers had said and protested current abuses. The best known among them was St. Thomas Aquinas. (*Go to: "St. Thomas Aquinas on Relics."*)

He also took a crack at justifying brandea—third-class relics—but emphasized this shouldn't be some kind of superstitious belief.

Enter the Protestants

That, of course, was an issue the Protestant reformers could really sink their teeth into. Some said all this relic business, which can't really be a business (*Go to: "The Sin of Simony"*), was flat-out idolatry; others said it was nothing but a Roman Catholic-invented moneymaker (and against Scripture). And still others only took shots at false relics.

That was why the Council of Trent had to address the issue. It didn't mention Scripture (but then, scriptural references to relics are pretty sparse and some would argue they don't exist at all), and instead said it was part of apostolic tradition and the constant practice of the Church. The bishops also seconded previous councils' condemnations of those who denied it was legal and proper to venerate relics.

In the seventeenth and eighteenth centuries, theologians had only a few comments on relics. One noted that when relics are reduced to nothing more than powder, it's "unbecoming"—

read "tacky"—to preserve them. Another said venerating relics wasn't equal to venerating saints. And a third taught that relics, in themselves, have no right to veneration but as representative of the saints (whose remains they are), they're worthy of the same veneration due the saint himself or herself. They only differ from the saint in that they can't move and they're not alive. Even so, he argued, they constitute one sole entity with the saint. That's why they deserve being shown the same dignity.

Bottom line for the Church: A relic as an object has value for sanctification insofar as it was once in direct contact with the saint. It can encourage holiness because of its association with a holy person.

In modern times—say, from the nineteenth century on—a lot of relics disappeared during revolutions, suppressions of churches and so on. On the other hand, new saints—new martyrs—have meant new relics. And these, unlike some of those earlier ones, are fully authenticated.

Advances in archaeology, historical research and science have also made authentication possible for earlier relics. But what about the pieces—once considered authentic—that we now know aren't? And what about items that have never been proven or disproven?

The Church says veneration of a traditional relic can continue even if it can't be authenticated. A lot of famous "relics" are—to quote a Catholic dictionary—"almost certainly spurious" (bogus), but "there is no need to assume deliberate fraud." Rather, "honor given in good faith to a false relic is nevertheless profitable to the worshipper and in no way dishonors the saint."

But, "relics proven and known to be false must be withheld from the people."

On the other hand, it adds, "no Catholic is formally bound

to the positive veneration of relics, but is forbidden by the Council of Trent to say that such veneration ought not to be given."

You don't have to be "into" relics but you can't say others shouldn't be.

In Our Own Time

Over the last two centuries, theologians have pretty much just repeated what was said at Trent when it came to justifying veneration of relics:

1) The bodies of saints are temples of the Holy Spirit.

2) They are members of the body of Christ.

3) They are destined for final resurrection.

That covers first-class relics. Theologians haven't been as quick to tackle second- and third-class even though both remain popular.

Vatican II mentions relics in its document on the liturgy: "The saints have been traditionally honored in the Church and their authentic relics and images held in veneration."

Period.

The *Catechism of the Catholic Church* says only "Besides sacramental liturgy and sacramentals, catechesis must take into account the forms of piety and popular devotions among the faithful. The religious sense of the Christian people has always found expression in various forms of piety surrounding the Church's sacramental life, such as the veneration of relics, visits to sanctuaries, pilgrimages, processions, the stations of the cross, religious dances, the rosary, medals, etc." [1674]."[11]

And the revised Code of Canon Law simply notes:

—"It is absolutely forbidden to sell sacred relics." (Simony.)

—"Significant relics or other ones which are honored with great veneration by the people cannot in any manner be validly alienated or perpetually transferred without the permission of the Apostolic See." (No moving a big-time relic without the Vatican's say-so.)

—"The [above] prescription is also applicable to images in any church which are honored with great veneration by the people." (Ditto with works of art.)

—And "the ancient tradition of keeping the relics of martyrs and other saints under a fixed altar is to be preserved according to the norms given in the liturgical books." (We haven't lost our "catacomb roots.")

A Box for Bones

A reliquary is the container in which relics are sealed and kept.

Some are nothing more than a simple box. Others are more like a casket. Most small relics—and some can be very, very small slivers or chips—are kept in a round case that has a stem and stand. These reliquaries look like miniature "monstrances"—the case, stem and stand used to display the consecrated host at Benediction and Eucharistic adoration.

A "portable" reliquary can be like a tiny "pyx"—looking like a small pocket watch or circular pill box.

The Not-So-Secret Catacombs

It's commonly believed that early Christians hid in the cata-combs to celebrate the Eucharist but historians say this isn't so. Yes, they prayed there, especially at a martyr's grave on the anniversary of his or her death, but the catacombs weren't some secret hideout.

So what were they? Underground burial spots, with cave-like vaults connected by chambers. The walls were carved out with niches and the bodies—sometimes two or three—laid to rest on a single shelf sealed off with a stone slab. Rich folks were buried alone in better spots, big enough to hold a sar-cophagus—a large stone coffin.

It wasn't just Rome that had catacombs, but Malta, Sicily, Asia Minor, North Africa and some places in Western Europe, too. But Rome's were—and are—the best known. There, soft tufa stone made digging easy.

Roman officials didn't mess with Christian graves because Romans didn't mess with graves.

In the fourth century, after Christianity was no longer ille-gal, Church leaders enlarged the chambers, especially the areas around popular martyrs. That only made sense. They had to accommodate the crowds coming on anniversaries. To further help, shafts were dug—called "luminaries"—to give more light and ventilation. (What we could call skylights, but in the ground.)

But, over time, the remains—the relics—were moved from the catacombs and into churches.

After the German invasions and through the Middle Ages, the catacombs were all but forgotten. In 1578, they were acci-dentally rediscovered, causing a buzz of renewed interest in them.

Altar Stones

Up until the Second Vatican Council, every altar, including portable ones, was required to have a tiny relic of a martyr sealed in its altar stone.

This was done to remind folks of the earlier practice of celebrating Mass over the tombs of the martyrs. Since Vatican II, new altars have a relic in them only if they are solid and attached to the floor of the church.

Moveable altars, such as those in most parishes, do not have an altar stone or a relic.

These days, in permanent altars, the relic is to be of substantial size, and it may be of any saint. The usual practice is to seal it inside the altar cavity rather than in the stone table top, which was the older practice.

St. Peter and St. Paul Come to North Carolina

Not long ago, the bishop of Raleigh, North Carolina, placed an incredible collection of saints' relics into the permanent altar at the renovated Sacred Heart Cathedral.

In fact, Peter and Paul arrived just in time for the ceremony. *The* Peter and Paul.

Relics from two of the most important saints in the Catholic Church came in minuscule envelopes, each sealed with a tiny red blob of wax. The envelopes, marked with "S. Petri Ap." and "S. Pauli Ap.," rested in a golden box, ready to be placed and sealed in the cathedral's new marble altar.

They joined relics of St. Matthew, St. Mark, St. Jude, St. Francis of Assisi, St. Elizabeth Ann Seton and others. All but two of the relics were sent to Raleigh by the Vatican.

Pastor Father Tim O'Connor said he knew he would need relics for the new altar so he asked the Vatican for help. He sent a list of names he was interested in, including Peter and Paul. "I thought I'd reach for the sky and see what I'd get," he said. "They sent them all."

The priest admits he has "connections" in the Vatican; his great-uncle is head canon at St. Peter's and he is friends with a nun who works in the Vatican and "knows all the people."

When the first shipment from the Vatican came, Peter and Paul were not among the relics, but Father O'Connor didn't really expect to get such a gift from Rome. When he called his contacts to thank them, however, they said that the two were on their way as well.

The relics arrived a couple of days before the scheduled liturgy, by regular mail.

"That's the part that just blew my mind," Father O'Connor said. "Regular mail."

St. Thomas Aquinas on Relics

In his *Summa Theologica*, St. Thomas Aquinas starts his teaching on relics by quoting St. Augustine:

"As Augustine says...: 'If a father's coat or ring, or anything else of that kind, is so much more cherished by his children, as love for one's parents is greater, in no way are the bodies themselves to be despised, which are much more intimately and closely united to us than any garment; for they belong to man's very nature.'"

(If we treasure an item that belonged to a dead loved

one, we aren't going to consider their mortal remains as worth less than that.)

"It is clear from this that he who has a certain affection for anyone, venerates whatever of his is left after his death, not only his body and the parts thereof, but even external things, such as his clothes, and such like."

(If we loved someone, we hold dear what belonged to her—not just her body but her personal possessions.)

"Now it is manifest that we should show honor to the saints of God, as being members of Christ, the children and friends of God, and our intercessors."

(That sentence is pretty straightforward.)

"Wherefore in memory of them we ought to honor any relics of theirs in a fitting manner: principally their bodies, which were temples, and organs of the Holy Spirit dwelling and operating in them, and are destined to be likened to the body of Christ by the glory of the Resurrection. Hence God Himself fittingly honors such relics by working miracles at their presence."

(We honor them by honoring their relics—their dead bodies—and we know God thinks highly of these relics because he works miracles through them.)

The Sin of Simony

Simony—forbidden by Church law—is the selling or buying of something spiritual like a grace, a sacrament or a relic.

It gets its name from Simon in the Acts of the Apostles (8:9-24). Not Simon Peter, the first pope. This Simon was a magician who converted to Christianity. When he saw what the apostles could do, he offered to pay them to give him the same abilities.

Bad plan, Simon. But it did make your name part of Christianity's vocabulary.

Ask St. Joe:
Where Did We Get Those Holy Names?

Dear St. Joe:

The U.S. Constitution insists on the separation of Church and State, so why are so many American cities and towns named for saints?

Citizen of St. Augustine, Florida

Dear Citizen:

A lot were named—by missionaries or religious groups—long before there was a U.S. Constitution. Others were chosen by the local community, and the folks there had a particular attraction toward that holy man or woman.

St. Joe

Quote / Unquote

"We honor the martyrs' relics, so that thereby we give honor to Him Whose martyrs [whose witnesses] they are: we honor the servants, that the honor shown to them may reflect on their Master."

—St. Jerome (c. 343–420)

CHAPTER EIGHT

Patrons: Getting By With a Little Help From Our Friends

Ask the Expert

It's tempting to think anything related to theology—anything associated with religion or spirituality—has some complicated, hard-to-understand basis. But that isn't always the case. Patron saints are a great example of how ordinary folks—people like you and like me—developed the custom of calling on deceased holy men, women and children for help.

Every era, since the time of the apostles, has had its holy people. Some were known only locally. Others, especially in our own time, have been recognized almost universally.

Mother Teresa is a good example. She began working in obscurity in the streets of Calcutta and ended up winning the Nobel Peace Prize. Her funeral was beamed on live television around the world.

It's true that while she was alive she couldn't be declared a saint, but few would argue she displayed many of the traits of sainthood. If Las Vegas had a line on canonizations, the smart money would be on her.

What did happen in our "global village" is her name became synonymous with holiness and with helping the poor. Countless television shows—from sitcoms to dramas—included some form of the line: "I'm no Mother Teresa."

And viewers knew *exactly* what the character meant, whether the words were delivered seriously or for laughs.

But what about folks who *want* to be like her? Those who want to develop their ability to love and to serve? Those who are working with the poor or considering working with the poor?

To whom could they turn for help? The answer is pretty obvious. Just as they flocked to hear her speak, to read her words, to join in her work while she was still living, they find their thoughts—their prayers—turning to her after she died. And in death—because of the communion of saints—she has the ability to intercede for them, to offer them help in ways she couldn't when she was still on the earth.

It's good to keep in mind that there's nothing extraordinary about asking an expert for aid. ("Yo! A little help here!") If I want to be a great cook, then I wouldn't pass up an opportunity to get one-on-one instruction from a world-class chef. If I want to improve my golf game, I would jump at the chance to attend a clinic run by the winner of this year's U.S. Open. When I want to get better at doing something or being something, I look to the people who are very, very good at doing that or being that.

It only makes sense.

One of Ours

The early Christians knew they might be arrested, tortured and killed. They also knew there were others—their peers—who had already successfully run that race (to use St. Paul's phrase from 2 Timothy 4:7). These were folks who didn't head for the hills, didn't renounce their faith in Jesus, didn't panic and abandon their deepest beliefs.

And how much more appealing was that person, that martyr, that saint, if he or she came from my own country? My own city? My own village? He was my bishop, my pastor. I knew her cousin. He or she and my grandparent were childhood friends.

Then, to my way of thinking, these are real people, more like me than unlike me. And not only can they inspire me by what they did, they can help me—right here, right now—become more willing to do what they did. I can call on them when I'm afraid of what the future might hold for me and for my loved ones. When I know torture and death are a possibility.

More than that, I'm proud of them. You know that famous martyr? I was born two blocks from where she was born. Her bones—her shrine—are in my town. She's one of us. She takes care of us.

But it wasn't just location that created a bond. It was also the other particulars of that man or woman. If she died a virgin at a young age, and I'm a young virgin, then there is an attraction to her. Where I am, she was. Where she is, I hope to someday be.

If he was a tentmaker, and I'm a tentmaker, then he's the saint for me. Here's a fellow who knows the ins and outs of my profession. Somebody who has a pretty good idea of what my life is like.

He fished for a living. She was a musician. He was a soldier. She was a devoted mother. The list goes on and on. (*Go to: "A Patron Sampler."*)

As the centuries passed, new saints meant new patrons. Not just martyrs but "confessors." (Technically, all "nonmartyrs.") And "mystics."

Then, too, the "translation" of remains—the moving of relics to other regions—could mean the "adoption" of a patron. This town might not have been the home of this particular saint or the place where he died, but because his relic is kept here, then he is its special helper. And the residents in that area know the story of his life and death. They're familiar with the miracles—some true, some perhaps only pious legends—attributed to him and to his remains.

As mentioned in chapter seven, that saint—that patron—was a focal point in civic life. Oaths were taken in her name. Her feast day was a great holiday with all kinds of celebrations, including a procession through the town with her relic leading the parade.

When the members of a particular guild—a particular profession—got together, they acknowledged the saint that was their patron. In the same way a town displayed its civic pride in "its" saint, and the workers claimed bragging rights to a particular holy man or woman somehow associated with their occupation.

Sometimes the choice was obvious and sometimes it was a little ... well, gruesome. It could be a patron wasn't chosen because of where he lived or what his work was, but because of how he was tortured or how he died.

St. Apollonia, the patron of dentists, had her teeth pulled out before being put to death in 249.

St. Lawrence, the patron of cooks, was killed on a red-hot griddle in 258. (Tradition says that in the middle of his suffering, he joked with his executioner that it was time to turn him over. He was done on that side.)

But even as kingdoms and professions claimed and called on patrons, individuals realized they had the ability to do the same. That was especially true when it came to health. In the Middle Ages, when science and medicine were primitive at best, a life span was short. Infant death was not uncommon. A simple cold could lead to pneumonia. A sliver or small cut could result in blood poisoning. Plague could decimate a region.

A Medieval H.M.O.

For centuries, the fourteen Holy Helpers were prayed to by countless Christians. (*Go to: "St. Blaise and the Fourteen Holy Helpers."*) They were seen as particular intercessors for dealing with a variety of calamities.

Like other saints, they were at times depicted artistically with their symbols. Not infrequently a patron—or any saint—had an object with which he or she was identified. A statue or figure in a stained-glass window could be any one of several dozen saints but the item he held or a characteristic of her appearance gave the identity. (A shamrock for St. Patrick, for example.)

And, certainly, during periods when literacy was uncommon, this way of recognizing a particular saint made great sense. (It could also be a subtle or not-so-subtle code or a thumbing of the nose at secular authority cracking down on the Church. After King Henry VIII clamped down on Roman Catholicism in sixteenth-century England, more than a few pubs named for saints altered their names but not their symbols.)

Patrons still have their appeal in our own time. A new parish chooses a particular saint who has a special meaning to its members. A long-time parish has a traditional pride in the man or woman for whom it's named. Children raised there feel a unique kinship to him or her.

More personally, the custom of naming a child for a saint continues. Yes, today there are more "non-saint" names but that's a trend Church leaders wouldn't mind curbing.

Naming a child for a saint is a natural way to encourage that little one to develop an interest in the saint and a particular devotion to him or her. But—again, on a personal level—individuals continue to be attracted to particular saints for particular reasons.

In a sense, they choose their own patron.

This has been going on throughout the history of the Church. Even the saints have had their favorite saints.

Picking a Patron

How is that connection made? It might be because of a namesake. Or a profession. It might be because of something the saint said or wrote that the person finds especially appealing, inspiring or relevant.

It might be because the person suffers from the same physical, mental or emotional illness as that saint did.

It might be because a mom or dad, a godparent or other influential adult had a devotion to that saint.

It might be because of a holy card, a statue, a stained glass window.

It might be the result of a heartfelt prayer mumbled in desperation. ("What have I got to lose?")

Somehow, somewhere, sometime, there is a connection. In human terms, a random (or maybe not so random) meeting that leads to a relationship. Then a friendship. And, finally, a deep love.

In simplest terms, a patron saint is one loved by a particular person (or people) for a particular reason. And one of the joys and pleasant challenges of being a Catholic can be finding that someone special. Knowing that he or she can offer help in this life and be a companion in the next.

A Patron Sampler

A complete list of patron saints would include hundreds and hundreds of names. And while some occupations, conditions or places have more than one patron, this sample list—for the most part—includes only one each. (You'll also see that a number of places have a particular devotion to Mary as their patroness.)

Occupations and Conditions

Accountants and bankers (and all IRS employees): Matthew. An obvious choice, this apostle/evangelist was a tax collector.

Animals: Francis of Assisi (1181–1226). His love for God's little creatures is still so well-known that his statue is a popular one in gardens.

Archers: Sebastian (died around 288). Sentenced to death, he was shot by archers but survived and was healed by Irene, the widow of the martyr St. Castulus. After the emperor got over his shock at this unexpected turn of events, he ordered Sebastian clubbed to death. Sebastian was a favorite image for painters and sculptors during the Renaissance.

Blind people: Odilia (died around 720). Born blind, she was given away by her parents. (Her mother had pleaded with her father—a local nobleman—that the disabled child should not just be put to death.) Later, after she entered a convent at age twelve, her sight was miraculously restored.

Blood banks: Januarius (died 304). A bishop and martyr whose blood—contained in a reliquary vial—is said to liquefy annually on his feast day, September 19. This phenomenon has been happening, and celebrated, for centuries.

Brides: Nicholas of Myra (died around 350). Yes, this is "St.

Nick," the original Santa Claus and patron of children. Tradition also says he saved three young women from prostitution by throwing bags of gold through their windows at night. Their father had been unable to provide dowries for them and so had planned for them to enter that profession.

Cabdrivers: Fiacre (died around 670). This hermit and miracle worker is associated with the cabs of Paris (called "fiacres") because the industry was founded near the Hotel Saint-Fiacre.

Cancer patients: Peregrine (1260–1345). After being a "dissolute youth"—to put it politely—he became a monk and mystic. (Tradition says he changed his wild-thing ways after he smacked St. Philip Benizi in the face during some public disturbance and Philip calmly turned the other cheek.) Later, he suffered cancer of the foot until, as a result of a vision, he was miraculously cured.

Carpenters: Joseph. Of course.

Emigrants: Frances Xavier Cabrini (1850–1917). Mother Cabrini emigrated from Italy to the United States and worked with immigrants in North and South America.

Fishermen: Andrew. Peter's brother and a fellow professional angler. (But why would golfers look to him as well? Because, laddie, he's the patron of Scotland, the birthplace of that grand and frustrating sport. And the most famous course there bears his name.)

Florists: Thérèse of Lisieux (1873–1897). "The Little Flower" promised to spend her heaven "doing good on earth," showering it with roses. Her admirers continue to cite miraculous interventions that—somehow or other—involve a rose.

Funeral directors: Joseph of Arimathea. Jesus' "undertaker" is an obvious choice.

Greetings: Valentine (died 269). The custom of sending

"Valentines" on his feast, February 14, dates back to the medieval belief that birds chose their mates on that day, making the priest, physician and martyr the patron of lovers.

Hairdressers: Martin de Porres (1579–1639). A mystic and miracle worker, he earned his keep as a young man by being a barber/surgeon. (There was more about him in chapter five.)

Heart patients: John of God (died 1550). Also the patron of the sick and hospitals, John founded the Brothers Hospitallers.

Housewives: Anne. As the mother of Mary, she's a good choice for patroness of grandmothers, too.

Lawyers: Thomas More (1478–1535). The lord chancellor of England, "the king's good servant, but God's first," was put to death by Henry VIII.

Librarians: Jerome (c. 341–420). He translated the Old Testament—the Jewish Scriptures—from Hebrew into Latin and revised the Latin version of the New Testament.

Lost or hopeless causes: Jude. (*Go to: "Hey, Jude!"*)

Mentally ill: Dymphna (mid-seventh century). Best known through legend, she was the daughter of a pagan Celtic chieftain. She took off after her widower father began taking a romantic interest in her. She left the country and founded an oratory (a place of prayer) but her father's soldiers tracked her down and, when she refused to return home, killed her. (Dymphna is also a good choice for patroness of those who suffer from depression and those who have been sexually abused.)

Messengers: Gabriel, the archangel who was God's messenger. (In fact, "angel" means "messenger.")

Mothers: Monica (332–387). Best known for the heartaches her son Augustine gave her prior to his conversion, Monica is also remembered for being a devoted wife (to a pretty crumb-bum husband) and loving daughter-in-law (to a mother-in-law who, at first, didn't like Monica at all). She's credited with converting both her husband and her mother-in-law..

Motorists: Christopher (died around 251). As mentioned in chapter five, he's the friend of all travelers.

Musicians: Gregory the Great (590–604). A scholar of many accomplishments, he's credited with the creation of a form of musical worship known as Gregorian chant.

Pawnbrokers: Nicholas. Remember those three sacks of gold? Tradition says the three balls on a pawnbroker's shop are a symbol of them.

Physicians: Luke. The doctor-evangelist.

Postal employees: Gabriel. Again, getting the message out.

Priests: John Vianney (1786–1859). This French parish priest was famous for hearing confessions.

Prisoners: Dismas. The "good thief" who died next to Christ.

Schools and students: Thomas Aquinas (1225–1274). One of the Church's greatest theologians and philosophers.

Scientists: Albert (c.1200–1280). He wrote on logic, the natural sciences, ethics, metaphysics, Scripture and theology. And he was Aquinas' teacher.

Searchers of lost articles: Anthony of Padua (died 1231). Actually, this Franciscan Doctor of the Church and "wonder worker" is patron of a number of places and people. Still, he's probably best known today for "finding" lost items. (A popular prayer is "Dear St. Anthony, please look around, something is lost and cannot be found ....")

Skiers and mountaineers: Bernard of Montjoux (died 1081). This bishop's diocese included Italy's alpine region. He built schools, hospitals and hospices up in the mountains. Two passes in the Alps are named for him. And, yes, the big dogs trace their name back to him, too.

Social workers: Louise de Marillac (1591–1660). A French widow, she opened her home to train workers for the poor and founded the Sisters (or Daughters) of Charity of St. Paul. She traveled throughout the country establishing orphanages, hospitals and other services for the destitute.

Television: Clare of Assisi (died 1253). A contemporary of St. Francis, she founded the Franciscan Poor Clares. Near the end of her life, she had a vision of the Mass from her bed. That was why, some seven centuries later, she was named the patroness of TV.

Youth: Aloysius Gonzaga (1568–1591). A brilliant scholar, Aloysius joined the fledgling Society of Jesus—the Jesuits—and died at an early age taking care of plague victims.

Places

Americas: . . . . .Our Lady of Guadalupe

Canada: . . . . .Joseph and Anne

England: . . . . .George

Europe: . . . . .Benedict, Cyril and Methodius,
Bridget of Sweden, Catherine of Siena
and Edith Stein

France: . . . . .Joan of Arc

Germany: . . . . .Boniface

Greece: . . . . .Nicholas

India: . . . . .Our Lady of the Assumption

Ireland: . . . . .Patrick, Brigid and Columba

Italy: . . . . .Francis of Assisi and Catherine of Siena

Japan: . . . . .Peter Baptist

Korea: . . . . .Joseph, and Mary, Mother of the Church

Mexico: . . . . .Our Lady of Guadalupe
Norway: . . . . .Olaf
Philippines: . . . . .Immaculate Heart of Mary
Poland: . . . . .Casimir
Russia: . . . . .Andrew
Scandinavia: . . . . .Ansgar
South America: . . . . .Rose of Lima
Spain: . . . . .James the Greater and Teresa of Avila
Sweden: . . . . .Bridget and Eric
United States: . . . . .Immaculate Conception

St. Blaise and the Fourteen Holy Helpers

Church historians say that in the middle of the fourteenth century, Christians began praying to a number of saints in what we might call a boxed set.

These were the fourteen Holy Helpers, designed to cover a variety of situations associated with the plague. Not wanting to be flip here, I suppose one could consider them a sort of spiritual first-aid kit. At a time when, often as not, the medical "cure" was as risky as the medical condition, it stands to reason these saints would be called on for help. (Then, too, as we know even in our own time, there are no medical cures for some illnesses.)

Praying to the fourteen Holy Helpers was particularly popular in Germany, and later the tradition spread to Hungary and Sweden. There's even a remnant of it today, a custom that faded some in the second half of the twentieth century but was going strong in the first.

Who was—is—on the "team"? Acacius, Barbara, Blaise, Catherine of Alexandra, Christopher, Cyriacus, Dionysius of Paris, Erasmus, Eustace, George, Margaret, Pantaleon, Vitus and Giles. While each has his or her own feast day, the group had its own, too (August 8), until 1969, when it was "suppressed."

Each also had a "specialty." Barbara for fever, Acacius for suffering during the final illness, George for the domestic animals that also contracted the plague, Pantaleon for physicians and Giles for the ability to make a final confession. The remainder were patrons for the many symptoms of the plague, including boils and dementia.

Which of the fourteen is most familiar to many Catholics today? Blaise.

In a custom that hasn't changed much in four centuries, folks come forward after Mass on his feast day—February 3—to have their throats blessed.

The priest holds two candles in the shape of an X which he places around each person's neck and prays: "Through the intercession of St. Blaise, bishop and martyr, may the Lord free you from evils of the throat and from any other evil."

How did a fourth-century bishop and martyr become associated with throats? Blaise was also a physician. Tradition says that while he was in prison, a mom brought her young son to him. The lad was in great pain because he had a fish bone caught in his throat. Blaise healed him.

Blaise also has a more gruesome patronage. He's the saint of "wool carders." A "card" is a toothed instrument used for cleaning and untangling wool before it's spun into thread. When the bishop refused to worship pagan gods, the local governor ordered his skin be ripped to shreds with iron cards. Later, he was beheaded.

Hey, Jude!

Historians say devotion to St. Jude as the patron of lost or hopeless causes was started in the United States.

In Chicago, in fact. At the end of the Roaring Twenties.

Folks had prayed to "the obscure" apostle before then but it wasn't until the Claretian Fathers at Our Lady of Guadalupe parish founded a shrine to him there that his popularity soared.

And unlike some saints, Jude didn't—and doesn't—have a special appeal to a particular country or ethnic group. He seems to be a favorite with everyone.

Researchers say there's no known reason why a shrine sprang up in Chicago in 1929—that no place claimed Jude—except for Claretian Father James Tort.

There had been a Claretian devotion to the apostle in Santiago, Chile, but that was pretty in-house. So, really, he was a great choice—the perfect saint—to start a devotion to because there was no devotion to him already. (One could start it without stepping on any other order's or shrine's toes.)

In those early days of the Great Depression, every pastor knew raising funds was a challenge and dioceses usually left clergy on their own to come up with the much-needed bucks.

That's not to say choosing St. Jude was part of some terribly clever marketing scheme. Truth be told, St. Jude chose the Claretians.

Shrine literature says Father Tort, a Claretian from Spain, came to the United States and in the mid-twenties was assigned to the Mexican community in Chicago. By that time he already had a personal devotion to St. Jude which he had acquired, almost by chance, when he was stationed in a church in Arizona. There he had come across a St. Jude holy card that may have been brought by migrants up from Central or South America.

He brought the card with him to the Windy City, and when he built Our Lady of Guadalupe Church he put in a statue of St. Jude. (He had to have it made special since none were available.)

He also put in a statue of the very popular St. Thérèse of Lisieux and said to both saints, "Whichever of you attracts the most attention, I will start a devotion to."

That could have caused some "territorial" problems because the Carmelites already had a strong devotion to St. Thérèse.

Parishioners began gravitating toward Jude, so during Holy Week Father Tort moved the Little Flower to a more obscure spot and put Jude the Obscure in hers.

Why does Jude carry that description—"obscure"—and how did he end up the patron of lost or hopeless causes? Some historians speculate that the apostle sometimes credited with writing one of the New Testament's epistles remained in the shadows because he had the misfortune of having a name very similar to Judas, his fellow apostle who betrayed Jesus.

And as for his relationship to hopeless causes … researchers just don't know, although there is speculation that it was the Claretians who decided on that. They point out that by the time he hit Chicago in 1929, they were promoting him that way.

Ask St. Joe:
I Want to Move This Property

Dear St. Joe:

Will you really stand on your head to help sell a house?
A Real Estate Agent

Dear Agent:

I assume you're referring to the now popular custom of burying a statue of me—upside down or right side up—in the yard of a home that's for sale. (In fact, some religious goods stores and catalogs have "St. Joseph Sales Kits.")

Let me say this: No one is sure how the tradition began and while it is a bit bizarre, if it's done in a prayerful way, why would I not help out? (But, please, after the sale is made, dig my statue back up.)

St. Joe

Quote / Unquote

"The holy synod enjoins on all bishops and others who sustain the office and charge of teaching that ... they especially instruct the faithful diligently concerning the intercession and invocation of saints; the honor paid to relics; and the legitimate use of images; teaching them that the saints, who reign together with Christ, offer up their own prayer to God for men; that it is good and useful suppliantly to invoke them, and to have recourse to their prayers, aid and help for obtaining benefits from God, through his Son Jesus Christ our Lord, Who alone is our Redeemer and Savior.... Also that the holy bodies of holy martyrs and others now living with Christ ... are to be venerated by the faithful, through which bodies many benefits are bestowed by God on men...."

—Decree of the Council of Trent,
Session 25,
December 1563

CHAPTER NINE

How to Become a Saint in Your Spare Time

Is it possible to become a saint in your spare time? That doesn't seem likely. But it can be the place where you start.

Maybe we need to begin thinking about sainthood—about holiness—in a different way. Rather than focusing on "I have to do this, this and this and I have to avoid that, that and that," we need to think of holiness as a relationship.

That's what it is, of course. It's our relationship—one on one—with God.

If that's the case, then, as with any relationship, it can start in our "spare" time but as it deepens and develops—as it becomes more important to us, more central to who we are and who we want to be—it's going to occupy more of our schedule.

But becoming a saint isn't just putting in time. Yes, it takes time but that's not the point any more than just putting in time is the point of a happy marriage. Maybe if we compare becoming a saint with becoming a loving spouse, sainthood will seem more possible. And more attractive.

Just as marriage is giving oneself freely to another, giving oneself selflessly to another, sainthood is giving oneself to God. It's moving toward the realization—perhaps without ever fully reaching it on earth—that I was created by God to love God. And to love is to give. (Because of God's love for us, we've been given life.)

How do I give? What does God want of me? Not of humanity, but of *me*. Singular.

If the saints teach us anything, it's that God loves us and wants to love others through us. He wants to use us—in countless ways—to help others discover and fall in love with him.

And, at the same time, being human beings just like us, the saints—it seems safe to speculate—would be quick to say, "If I can do it, anyone can. I'm not special. I'm no different than you. Except …

"Except for my relationship with God, and he offers the exact same thing to you."

His infinite love.

It's yours for the asking. For the taking. For the sharing.

And as we begin to ask, begin to take, begin to share, we become better at recognizing God. We catch a glimpse of him in the hungry. In the thirsty. In the stranger. In the naked and the imprisoned. Jesus says (in Matthew 25:31-46) that when we help the needy among us, we're helping him.

And when we ignore them or forget about them, we're ignoring and forgetting about him.

And it's on this that we—each of us—will be judged.

But—and this is important—we can't judge other people and we can't compare ourselves to other people. It doesn't seem accidental that in Matthew, just before Jesus talks about the poor and needy, he tells his disciples the parable of the talents.

Matthew 25:14-30 says God gives each of us different gifts. (A "talent" is the name of coin.) To one he gives five, to another two and to a third only one. We're expected to use whatever we've been given.

God wants a good return on his investment.

We aren't supposed to be afraid of developing and using

God's gifts. We aren't supposed to squander them.

And we can't compare what we have—what we do—with what someone else has or is able to do. As we've seen in this book, some saints were Doctors of the Church, popes, royalty and founders of great religious orders. And some were gatekeepers. Some were geniuses. And some—if they had lived in our own time—might have been in special ed.

We aren't supposed to "bury" our talents whether we've been given five, two or one. We're supposed to use them ... for what?

For finding our way to God. For becoming saints.

That's what a saint is, after all. Some are canonized, some aren't. But every soul in heaven is a saint and that's why we were created. Made out of love to love. To spend eternity with Love.

Face-to-face.

As the Church prays at the end of the Mass on November 1, the Feast of All Saints:

"God is the glory and joy of all his saints,
whose memory we celebrate today.
May his blessings be with you always. Amen.

"May the prayers of the saints deliver you from present evil:
may their example of holy living
turn your thoughts to the service of God and neighbor.
    Amen.

"God's holy Church rejoices that her children
are one with the saints in lasting peace.
May you come to share with them
in all the joys of our Father's house. Amen."

Amen.

—November 1, 1999

Notes

1. cf. *LG*, 40; 48-51.
2. Nicetas, *Expl. symb.* 10: PL 52:871B.
3. St. Thomas Aquinas, Symb. 10.
4. *Indulgentiarum doctrina,* 5.
5. *Indulgentiarum doctrina,* 5.
6. Cf. Council of Trent (1551): DS 1712-1713; (1563): 1820.
7. CF GS 13§ 1.
8. CF. Council of Trent: DS 1513; Pius XII: DS 3897; Paul VI: AAS 58 (1966), 654.
9. Lateran Council IV (1215): DS 800.
10. Rom 8:28.
11. Cf. Council of NiceaII: DS 601; 603; Council of Trent: DS 1822.

Index